Big Sur Coast
Travel Guide 2023

Traveler's Geotag Handbook

Destiny Brian

Table of Contents

Introduction

Welcome to a world where sky and sea collide in a fascinating dance of colors. The Big Sur Coast stretches for approximately 90 miles along the famous Pacific Coast Highway (Highway 1), showcasing a diverse range of landscapes that are sure to leave you awe-struck. From the rugged cliffs of Bixby Creek Bridge to the iconic McWay Falls tumbling onto the pristine sands, every twist and turn of the highway reveals a new postcard-worthy view.

settled along the attractive coastline of California, the Big Sur Coast stands as a testament to nature's grandeur and beauty. A destination that has captured the hearts of artists, adventurers, and wanderers alike, Big Sur offers an unparalleled blend of rugged cliffs, serene beaches, and lush forests. This travel guide is your key to unlocking the secrets of this coastal treasure , providing you with the essential information and insights to make your journey through Big Sur an unforgettable experience.

Geotag Information:
Latitude: 36.3615° N
Longitude: 121.8563° W

Nature enthusiasts will find themselves in paradise as they tour the intricate network of state parks that dot the coastline. Pfeiffer Big Sur State Park offers a tapestry of redwood groves, waterfalls, and hiking trails, while Julia Pfeiffer Burns State Park boasts the ethereal McWay Falls and an array of trails that offer panoramic vistas. Point Lobos State Natural Reserve, a short drive north, offers a chance to witness the diverse marine life of the Pacific Ocean through tide pools and rugged shoreline.

For those seeking tranquility, Big Sur's hidden beaches beckon. Limekiln State Park's secluded coves and Redwood Creek Beach's mystical ambiance provide the perfect backdrop for relaxation. Adventurous spirits can tourthe Cone Peak area, where rugged trails lead to breathtaking vistas from atop the Santa Lucia Mountains. Additionally, the Sykes Hot Springs trail offers a challenging hike rewarded by the soothing embrace of natural hot springs deep within the wilderness.

dip yourself in the local culture by visiting the Henry Miller Memorial Library, a tribute to the American author who found inspiration in the region. The library hosts cultural events, live music, and showcases local art, making it a hub for creative expression. As you traverse the coastline, be sure to sample the region's delectable cuisine at iconic spots like Nepenthe, where you can savor a meal while overlooking the Pacific. Don't miss out on the chance to tour the local art galleries and boutique shops that feature the works of talented artisans.

Whether you're embarking on a soul-searching journey, a romantic getaway, or an adventure with friends, the Big Sur Coast promises an experience like no other. From the ethereal sunrise at Bixby Creek Bridge to the vibrant hues of sunset reflecting off the cliffs, every moment here is an invitation to connect with nature's splendor. This travel guide is your compass to navigate the wonders of Big Sur, ensuring that your visit to this coastal haven is brimming with unforgettable memories and a deep appreciation for the majesty of the natural world.

Overview

The Big Sur Coast, settled along California's rugged Pacific coastline, is a natural wonderland that beckons travelers seeking breathtaking landscapes, outdoor adventures, and serene getaways. This travel guide serves as your companion to tour this iconic destination.

Getting There: Before embarking on your Big Sur adventure, plan your journey. Accessible by car from major California cities like San Francisco and

Los Angeles, the Pacific Coast Highway (Highway 1) is the main route. Alternatively, you can arrive by air at Monterey Regional Airport.

When to Visit: The best time to visit Big Sur is from late spring to early fall, when mild weather prevails. Be mindful of potential road closures during the rainy season due to landslides.

Accommodations: Big Sur offers a variety of lodging options, from rustic cabins and campgrounds to luxurious resorts perched atop cliffs. Popular choices include Ventana Big Sur, Post Ranch Inn, and campgrounds within Pfeiffer Big Sur State Park.

Things to Do

Scenic Drives

Pacific Coast Highway: Drive along this iconic route for fascinating coastal views.
Bixby Creek Bridge: Stop at this photographic spot for a classic Big Sur photo.

Hiking and Nature
Julia Pfeiffer Burns State Park: tourMcWay Falls and the Ewoldsen Trail.

Pfeiffer Big Sur State Park: Hike among towering redwoods in this lush forest.

Beaches:

Pfeiffer Beach: Known for its purple sands and Keyhole Arch.
Andrew Molera State Park: A peaceful beach for picnics and tidepooling.

Wildlife Watching:

Whale Watching: Spot migrating whales from various viewpoints.
Condor Viewing: Visit the Ventana Wildlife Society's Discovery Center.

Dining:

Nepenthe: Savor panoramic ocean views with a diverse menu.
Big Sur Bakery: Enjoy artisanal bread and pastries in a pleasant setting.

Art Galleries:

Hawthorne Gallery: tourlocal and contemporary art.

Coast Gallery Big Sur: Admire unique artwork inspired by the region.

Spa Retreats:

Esalen Institute: Experience healing hot springs and holistic therapies.
Ventana Big Sur: Unwind with a spa treatment overlooking the Pacific.

Safety Tips: Stay hydrated and pack essentials for outdoor activities.
Regard nature and stick to Leave No Trace standards.

Big Sur Coast is a haven for those seeking awe-inspiring natural beauty, outdoor adventures, and relaxation. Whether you're a nature enthusiast, a foodie, or simply in search of tranquility, this guide will help you make the most of your visit to this iconic destination along the California coast.

Geography and Climate

Geography: The Big Sur Coast is a breathtaking destination that beckons travelers with its awe-inspiring landscapes, dramatic cliffs, and pristine natural beauty. This remote stretch of coastline, extending approximately 90 miles from

Carmel to San Simeon, is a haven for nature enthusiasts, adventure seekers, and those in search of tranquility amidst the wild. In this travel guide, we will embark on a journey to tour the geography of Big Sur Coast, revealing its stunning features and providing you with insights to make the most of your visit.

Geographic Location: Big Sur Coast is situated in Monterey County, California, and it's a part of the larger Central Coast region. It's conveniently located along California's iconic Highway 1, making it accessible to travelers driving from both San Francisco to the north and Los Angeles to the south.

Terrain and Topography: The defining characteristic of Big Sur Coast is its rugged and dramatic topography. Towering cliffs rise dramatically from the Pacific Ocean, reaching heights of over 1,000 feet in some places. These cliffs are often adorned with vibrant wildflowers during the spring and summer months, creating a vivid contrast against the deep blue of the ocean below.

Vegetation and Flora: Big Sur Coast boasts a diverse range of plant life. Coastal redwoods, known as some of the tallest trees on Earth, thrive in the region's moist climate. Inland, you'll find oak woodlands and chaparral-covered hillsides. The wildflower displays in the spring and early summer are a sight to behold, with blooms of lupine, poppies, and California lilac carpeting the landscape.

Wildlife: The rugged terrain and protected status of many areas along the coast have created a haven for wildlife. Keep an eye out for California condors soaring overhead, sea otters frolicking in the kelp forests just offshore, and, if you're lucky, migrating gray whales making their way along the coastline.

Notable Landmarks:

Bixby Creek Bridge: This iconic bridge spans a deep canyon and offers one of the most photographed views along Highway 1.

McWay Falls: A rare "tidefall" that cascades directly into the ocean, creating a stunning vista.

Pfeiffer Big Sur State Park: A gateway to the redwood forests with miles of hiking trails.

Julia Pfeiffer Burns State Park: Home to McWay Falls and pristine coastal views.

Activities:
Hiking, camping, and photography are some of the most popular activities on the Big Sur Coast. Trails like the Ewoldsen Trail and the Pine Ridge Trail offer opportunities to tour the region's rugged beauty. For a more leisurely experience, visit the pleasant art galleries and boutique shops in the village of Big Sur.

Big Sur Coast is a geographic wonderland, where the meeting of land and sea creates a symphony of natural beauty. Whether you seek adventure or tranquility, this coastal Treasure promises an unforgettable journey through its stunning geography. Plan your trip wisely, for in Big Sur, nature's grandeur awaits at every turn, inviting you to be a part of its breathtaking tapestry.

Climate: The Big Sur Coast offers a unique and fascinating climate that's essential for travelers to understand when planning their visit. This region is renowned for its breathtaking natural beauty, and its climate plays a pivotal role in shaping the experiences of those who venture here.

Seasonal Variation: Big Sur experiences a Mediterranean climate characterized by distinct seasons. Each season brings its own beauty, so choosing when to visit depends on your preferences.

Spring (March - May): Spring is a fantastic time to visit, with mild temperatures and lush, green landscapes.

Average temperatures range from 50°F (10°C) to 70°F (21°C).

Wildflowers bloom, and waterfalls cascade down the cliffs, creating an attractive setting for hikers and nature enthusiasts.

Summer (June - August): Summer is the peak tourist season, thanks to warm and sunny weather.

Daytime temperatures typically range from 60°F (15°C) to 80°F (27°C), making it perfect for outdoor activities like hiking, camping, and beachcombing.

Be prepared for some crowds and higher accommodation prices during this time.

Fall (September - November): Fall offers a tranquil escape with mild weather and fewer crowds.

Average temperatures range from 50°F (10°C) to 75°F (24°C).

The foliage turns vibrant shades of red and gold, creating a stunning backdrop for those fascinating the region.

Winter (December - February): Winter in Big Sur is a quieter time, ideal for those seeking solitude.
Temperatures range from 45°F (7°C) to 60°F (15°C), but can occasionally drop lower.
Rainfall is more frequent, making the creeks flow and the landscape lush and green.

Rainfall: Rainfall is essential for the lushness of Big Sur. Most of the rain falls between November and April, with January being the wettest month. This is when waterfalls are at their most impressive, and the landscape is vibrant.

Coastal Influence: The Pacific Ocean greatly influences Big Sur's climate. Coastal areas are milder and more humid, while inland areas experience greater temperature fluctuations. The ocean's proximity means that fog is common, especially in the mornings, creating a mystical atmosphere.

Packing Tips: Dress in layers to accommodate temperature variations.
Comfortable walking shoes are essential for fascinating the diverse terrain.
Don't forget a waterproof jacket during the wetter months.

Whether you seek a sunny beach getaway or a serene retreat in nature, understanding Big Sur's climate is key to planning a memorable trip. This coastal Treasure invites visitors year-round, each season offering a unique and awe-inspiring experience. So, pack your bags and dip yourself in the breathtaking beauty of Big Sur's ever-changing climate.

History and Culture

History: The Big Sur Coast, is a destination that beckons adventurers and nature enthusiasts from around the world. This rugged and dramatic coastline, extending roughly from Carmel to San Simeon, is steeped in history, natural beauty, and a sense of awe-inspiring wonder.

Pre-European Settlement: Long before European settlers arrived, the indigenous Esselen and Ohlone people called Big Sur home. They thrived in this bountiful land, harvesting acorns, hunting, and crafting canoes from redwood trees that towered along the coast. Evidence of their presence can still be found in the form of shell middens and cave paintings.

Spanish Exploration: Big Sur's history took a new turn with the arrival of Spanish explorers. In 1769,

Gaspar de Portolà and his expedition became the first Europeans to gaze upon this breathtaking coastline. Spanish missions, such as San Carlos Borromeo de Carmelo Mission, were established in the region, bringing with them European influences and architecture.

American Settlement: In the mid-19th century, Big Sur saw an influx of American settlers who established ranches, logging operations, and small communities. These hardy pioneers endured isolation and rugged living conditions. One notable figure was John B. Post, who built the first wagon road connecting the region to Monterey.

Literary Inspiration: Big Sur's allure captivated literary giants like Henry Miller and Jack Kerouac in the 20th century. Kerouac's novel, "Big Sur," famously captured the area's mystique and rugged beauty. Their writings contributed to the region's growing reputation as a refuge for artists and free spirits.

Environmental Conservation: As the 20th century progressed, the need to protect Big Sur's unparalleled beauty became evident. In 1964, the area was designated a National Scenic Byway, and in 1967, it was further safeguarded as a state-protected coastal zone. These actions ensured the preservation of the region's pristine landscapes.

Modern Attractions: Today, Big Sur remains a haven for outdoor enthusiasts. Travelers are drawn to iconic landmarks like McWay Falls, Bixby Creek Bridge, and Pfeiffer Beach. Hiking trails, such as the famed McWay Falls Trail and the rugged Ventana Wilderness trails, offer experiences ranging from easy strolls to challenging backpacking adventures.

Cultural Festivals: Big Sur has also become a hub for cultural events. The Henry Miller Memorial Library hosts concerts, readings, and art exhibitions. Additionally, the Big Sur International Marathon attracts runners from all over the globe.

Culinary Delights: Food lovers won't be disappointed either. The region boasts acclaimed restaurants like Nepenthe, where you can savor local cuisine while overlooking the Pacific Ocean.

The history of the Big Sur Coast is a tapestry woven with the threads of indigenous cultures, Spanish exploration, American pioneering spirit, literary inspiration, and environmental conservation. Today, it continues to be a place where travelers can connect with nature's grandeur and a rich cultural heritage that has been lovingly preserved. Whether you're seeking adventure, relaxation, or artistic inspiration, Big Sur invites tourists to rugged shores and timeless beauty.

Culture: settled along the rugged coastline of California, Big Sur is a destination that beckons travelers seeking solace, inspiration, and a taste of the extraordinary. Beyond its breathtaking landscapes, Big Sur boasts a unique and enigmatic culture that is as fascinating as its natural beauty. In this travel guide, we will delve into the multifaceted culture of Big Sur Coast, providing you with an elaborate and detailed glimpse into this remarkable destination.

Artistic Expression: Big Sur has long been a haven for artists, writers, and creatives seeking inspiration from its dramatic vistas. The culture here thrives on artistic expression. You can tourthis by visiting local galleries such as the Hawthorne Gallery, which showcases contemporary art inspired by the region. The Henry Miller Memorial Library pays tribute to the legendary writer who once called Big Sur home, hosting literary events and art exhibitions.

Music and Festivals: Music pulses through the veins of Big Sur's culture. The Big Sur Folk

Festival and Big Sur Jazz Festival are annual events that draw musicians and music enthusiasts from around the world. These festivals embody the spirit of Big Sur, where music merges with the natural surroundings, creating an unforgettable experience.

Sustainable Living: A core facet of Big Sur's culture is its commitment to sustainable living. The community places a strong emphasis on environmental conservation, and you'll find eco-friendly practices integrated into daily life. Local businesses often prioritize sustainability, and you can visit places like the Big Sur Bakery, which sources ingredients locally and uses organic products.

Spirituality and Wellness: Big Sur has long been associated with spiritual retreats and wellness practices. The Esalen Institute, perched on the cliffs, offers workshops in yoga, meditation, and holistic healing. Visitors come to rejuvenate their minds and spirits amidst the serenity of the coastline.

Native American Heritage: The indigenous Esselen people have a deep-rooted history in Big Sur. You can learn about their heritage at the Salinan and Costanoan Indian Research Center. The culture of Big Sur pays homage to this history, with some businesses integrating indigenous practices and art into their operations.

Environmental Conservation:

Environmentalism is a way of life in Big Sur. The culture here promotes responsible tourism, with an emphasis on Leave No Trace principles. Local organizations work tirelessly to protect the fragile ecosystem, and you can participate in volunteer programs to give back to this pristine environment.

Culinary Delights: Big Sur's culinary scene is a fusion of flavors that reflect the region's culture. Restaurants like Nepenthe offer not only delectable cuisine but also breathtaking views of the coastline. Fresh seafood, farm-to-table dining, and a commitment to organic ingredients are staples of the local food culture.

Big Sur Coast isn't just a destination; it's an immersion into a distinctive culture shaped by its natural surroundings and the people who call it home. From artistic expression to sustainable living, music festivals to spiritual retreats, this coastal Treasure offers an enriching and enlightening experience for travelers. Embrace the culture of Big Sur, and you'll discover a world where nature and humanity coexist in perfect harmony, leaving an indelible mark on your soul.

Travel Tips and Advice

Traveling to Big Sur Coast is a magnificent experience, offering breathtaking coastal vistas, lush forests, and a serene escape from city life. Here's an elaborate guide with travel tips and advice for a memorable trip:

Plan Ahead: Research the best time to visit. Late spring and early fall are often ideal due to milder weather and fewer crowds.
Make accommodation reservations well in advance, as options are limited and fill up quickly.

Weather Awareness: Big Sur's climate can be unpredictable. Layer your clothing to adapt to temperature changes, and always carry a rain jacket.

Travel Routes: The iconic Highway 1 runs through Big Sur, offering stunning views. However, be prepared for winding roads and narrow stretches.
Check road conditions before your trip, as landslides and closures can occur.

Accommodations: Options range from rustic campsites to luxurious resorts. Choose according to your preference and budget.

Camping permits are essential for state parks like Pfeiffer Big Sur and Julia Pfeiffer Burns.

Wildlife and Nature:

Respect the wildlife; Do not approach or feed them. Keep a safe distance.

Stay on marked trails to preserve the fragile ecosystem and avoid poison oak.

Hiking: Big Sur boasts incredible hiking trails. Popular choices include McWay Falls Trail and Ewoldsen Trail.

Always carry a trail map, plenty of water, and wear appropriate footwear.

Photography: Big Sur is a photographer's dream. Capture sunrise and sunset moments, but also tourthe area during different times of the day for unique lighting.

Cell Service: Expect limited cell reception in many parts of Big Sur. Inform someone about your plans and whereabouts before venturing into remote areas.

Supplies: Stock up on groceries and essentials before arriving, as grocery stores can be scarce.

Dining: Enjoy local cuisine in pleasant restaurants like Nepenthe. Reservations are a good idea for popular spots.

Leave No Trace: Follow the Leave No Trace principles: pack out all trash, stay on established trails, and avoid disturbing the environment.

Safety: Be cautious near cliffs and steep drops, especially when taking photos.
Carry a first-aid kit and know the location of the nearest medical facilities.

Stargazing: Big Sur offers incredible stargazing opportunities. Bring binoculars or a telescope for an enhanced experience.

Respect Locals: Be mindful of the local community. Keep noise levels down, and drive carefully through residential areas.

Permits: Check if permits are required for any activities, such as campfires or special events, and obtain them as needed.

Waste Disposal: Dispose of waste properly. Many areas have limited restroom facilities, so plan accordingly.

Emergency Preparedness: Have a basic understanding of how to respond to emergencies, including wildfires or medical issues.

Maps and Navigation: Bring physical maps or a GPS device. Cell phone navigation can be unreliable.

Relax and Enjoy: The beauty of Big Sur lies in its serenity. Take your time, unplug, and savor the natural surroundings.

Remember, Big Sur is a place of immense natural beauty and tranquility. Respecting the environment and being prepared will ensure a safe and unforgettable journey along the stunning Big Sur Coast.

Chapter One: Planning Your Trip

Best Time to Visit

The best time to travel to the Big Sur Coast as a tourist or traveler depends on your preferences and what you hope to experience during your visit. Here's description of the different seasons and their advantages:

Spring (March to May):

Scenic Beauty: Spring is a fantastic time to visit for lush green landscapes, colorful wildflowers, and flowing waterfalls.

Moderate Weather: The weather is mild and comfortable, with temperatures ranging from 50°F to 70°F (10°C to 21°C).

Wildlife: Spring is when you can spot migrating whales, seals, and a variety of bird species along the coast.

Crowds: It's less crowded compared to summer, making it ideal for a peaceful getaway.

Summer (June to August):

Warmest Weather: Summer offers the warmest temperatures, ranging from 60°F to 80°F (15°C to 27°C), making it perfect for beach activities.

Clear Skies: Expect clear skies, which are ideal for outdoor adventures and stargazing.

Popular Time: However, it's the peak tourist season, so accommodations can be pricier, and some areas may be crowded.

Fall (September to November):

Mild Weather: Fall offers pleasant weather, with temperatures ranging from 50°F to 70°F (10°C to 21°C).

Foliage: Witness the stunning fall foliage as trees change color, creating a beautiful contrast against the coastline.

Fewer Crowds: Crowds begin to thin out after summer, allowing for a more tranquil experience.

Winter (December to February):

Dramatic Scenery: Winter provides a unique experience with dramatic stormy seas, rain-soaked cliffs, and misty coastal views.

Whale Watching: It's also an excellent time for whale watching, especially gray whales.

Cool and Wet: However, be prepared for cool and wet conditions, with temperatures ranging from 40°F to 60°F (4°C to 15°C).

Limited Amenities: Some facilities and accommodations may have reduced hours or close during this season.

The best time to travel to the Big Sur Coast depends on your preferences. If you want pleasant weather and vibrant landscapes, spring and fall are great choices. For warm beach days, summer is ideal, albeit busier. If you're after a unique and moody experience, winter offers dramatic scenery. Consider your interests and crowd tolerance when planning your visit to this breathtaking coastal destination.

Passport and Visa Requirements

Big Sur Coast offers a fantastic adventure. Here's a description of the passport and visa requirements for tourists and travelers:

Passport Requirements:

Validity: Ensure your passport is valid for at least six months beyond your planned departure date from the United States. Many countries enforce this rule.

Blank Pages: Your passport should have several blank pages for entry and exit stamps. It's generally recommended to have at least two blank pages.

Visa Waiver Program (VWP): If you're from a Visa Waiver Program country (like the UK, Germany, or Australia), you can visit the U.S. for tourism-related purposes for up to 90 days without a visa.
However, you need to obtain an ESTA (Electronic System for Travel Authorization) before your trip.

Non-VWP Countries: If your country is not in the VWP, you will need to apply for a B-2 tourist visa at the nearest U.S. embassy or consulate. This process typically includes an interview and requires documentation demonstrating the purpose of your visit and ties to your home country.

Visa Requirements:

ESTA (Electronic System for Travel Authorization): If you're eligible for the Visa Waiver Program, you must apply for an ESTA online before your trip. It's recommended to apply at least 72 hours before your departure. An approved ESTA is valid for multiple visits within two years or until your passport expires.

B-2 Tourist Visa: If you're not from a VWP country or your visit exceeds 90 days, you must apply for a B-2 tourist visa. The process includes completing the DS-160 form, paying the visa application fee, scheduling an interview at the nearest U.S. embassy or consulate, and attending the interview with the required documents.

Supporting Documents: Regardless of your visa category, you should carry essential documents such as a round-trip ticket, proof of accommodation in Big Sur, travel insurance, proof of sufficient funds for your stay, and a detailed itinerary of your trip.

Biometric Data: Travelers applying for U.S. visas may be required to provide biometric data, including fingerprints and digital photographs, during the application process.

Customs Regulations: Familiarize yourself with U.S. customs regulations, including what items are restricted or prohibited from entry.

It's crucial to verify the most up-to-date information on the official website of the U.S. Department of State or consult the nearest U.S. embassy or consulate in your home country as you are planning your trip to Big Sur Coast. Additionally, ensure you have travel insurance and any necessary vaccinations before traveling.

Travel Essentials

Here's a description of travel essentials for a trip to the Big Sur Coast, perfect for a travel guide for tourists and travelers:

Clothing:

Layers: Big Sur's weather can be unpredictable. Pack layers including lightweight clothing for warm days and warmer options for cool evenings.
Rain Jacket: Prepare for unexpected rain, especially in the winter months.
Comfortable Shoes: Sturdy hiking shoes are a must if you plan to tour the trails.

Camping Gear (if applicable):

Tent: If you're camping, a reliable tent is essential. Reserve campsites in advance.
Sleeping Bag and Pad: Stay warm and comfortable during nights in the great outdoors.
Cooking Gear: Portable stoves and cookware if you plan to cook your meals.

Maps and Navigation:

Maps and GPS: Cell service can be spotty, so have physical maps and a GPS device.

Trail Maps: If hiking, get detailed trail maps to navigate safely.

Food and Water:

Water Bottles: Carry sufficient water for your daily needs, especially on hikes.

Non-Perishable Food: High-energy snacks and easy-to-cook meals for camping trips.

Camping Permits and Reservations:

Campground Reservations: Book campsites well in advance, especially during peak seasons.

Backcountry Permits: If you plan on backcountry camping, acquire the necessary permits.

Safety Gear:

First Aid Kit: Basic medical supplies for emergencies.

Flashlight/Headlamp: Essential for navigating at night.

Whistle: For attracting attention if needed.

Electronics:

Portable Charger: Keep your devices charged, but use them sparingly to disconnect and enjoy nature.
Camera: Capture the breathtaking scenery.

Personal Items:

Sun Protection: Sunscreen, sunglasses, and a wide-brimmed hat to shield from the sun.
Toiletries: Basic toiletries and a biodegradable soap to minimize environmental impact.

Insect Repellent: Especially important for evening activities.
Identification: Carry identification and any necessary permits.

Leave No Trace Principles:

Trash Bags: Pack out all trash and litter.
Biodegradable Products: Use environmentally friendly products whenever possible.
Respect Wildlife: Keep a safe distance from animals and don't feed them.

Local Guidebooks:

Travel Guidebook: Learn about the history, culture, and must-visit spots in Big Sur.

Reservations and Permits:

Dining Reservations: Some restaurants require reservations due to limited seating.
State Park Pass: Consider purchasing a California State Parks pass for discounted park access.

Budget Planning:

Cash and Cards: Bring sufficient funds, including cash for places that don't accept cards.

COVID-19 Precautions (if applicable):

Face Masks: Follow local guidelines regarding mask usage.
Vaccination Proof: Keep copies of vaccination records if required.

Big Sur is known for its natural beauty, so respecting the environment and local guidelines is crucial for preserving this pristine destination. Always check the latest travel advisories and conditions before your trip for a safe and enjoyable adventure along the Big Sur Coast.

Budgeting and Costs

Big Sur Coast offers breathtaking views, attractive landscapes, and an unforgettable experience. To ensure your trip goes smoothly, it's essential to plan your budget carefully.

Transportation Costs:

Flights: The nearest major airport is Monterey Regional Airport (MRY). Flight costs vary depending on your departure location.
Car Rental: Consider renting a car for flexibility. Rates depend on the vehicle type and rental duration.

Accommodation Costs:

Hotels: Big Sur offers a range of lodging options, from luxury resorts to budget-friendly cabins. Prices vary greatly depending on the type of accommodation.
Camping: If you prefer camping, state parks like Pfeiffer Big Sur State Park have campgrounds. Per-night fees apply.

Food and Dining:

Restaurants: Big Sur boasts excellent dining options. Expect to spend between $20-60 per person for meals at restaurants, depending on the place's class.

Groceries: If you're on a tight budget, consider buying groceries in nearby towns like Monterey or Carmel and cooking your meals.

Activities and Sightseeing:

State Park Fees: Some state parks require entrance fees, typically around $10-15 per vehicle.

Tours: Costs for guided tours, such as whale watching or hiking excursions, can vary. Be sure to check in advance.

Fuel Costs: Gasoline prices fluctuate but plan for higher prices in remote areas like Big Sur. Consider fuel-efficient vehicles for long drives.

Miscellaneous Expenses:

Souvenirs: Budget for souvenirs and local art pieces if desired.

Emergency Funds: Always have a buffer for unexpected expenses.

Travel Insurance: It's advisable to have travel insurance to cover unforeseen circumstances.

Seasonal Considerations: Prices can vary by season. Summers are peak tourist times, while winters can be quieter and potentially cheaper.

Budgeting Tips: Research and book in advance for the best deals.
Consider camping to save on accommodation costs.
Pack essentials, as prices for items in Big Sur may be higher.

While Big Sur is known for its natural beauty, it's essential to plan your budget carefully. Costs can vary widely depending on your choices, but with thoughtful planning, you can enjoy this enchanting destination within your means.

Remember that costs can fluctuate, so it's wise to check the latest prices and availability before your trip. Enjoy your adventure along the stunning Big Sur Coast.

Itinerary Planning

Planning an itinerary for a trip to Big Sur Coast can be an exciting adventure. Big Sur is known for its rugged coastline, breathtaking views, and outdoor activities. Here's an elaborate itinerary to help you make the most of your visit:

Day 1: Arrival in Big Sur

Arrive at Monterey Regional Airport or drive in from nearby cities like San Francisco or Los Angeles.

Check into your chosen accommodation, whether it's a campsite, cabin, or a boutique hotel with ocean views.

Spend your evening relaxing and enjoying the local cuisine at a nearby restaurant. Consider trying fresh seafood dishes.

Day 2: Coastal Drive and Bixby Creek Bridge

Start your day with a scenic drive along Highway 1, one of the most iconic coastal routes in the world.

Stop at Bixby Creek Bridge, an iconic photo spot. Take in the beautiful scene and snap some photographs. tourPoint Lobos State Natural Reserve for hiking and wildlife viewing. Don't forget your camera!

Have a picnic lunch at one of the many scenic spots overlooking the Pacific Ocean.

Day 3: Hiking and Nature Exploration

Head to Julia Pfeiffer Burns State Park to see McWay Falls, an attractive waterfall that drops onto a beach.

Hike the Ewoldsen Trail in Julia Pfeiffer Burns State Park for an immersive redwood forest experience.

Visit Pfeiffer Beach with its famous purple sand and Keyhole Rock, best for sunset photography.

Relax and unwind at your accommodation in the evening.

Day 4: Adventure Activities

For the adventurous, consider booking a kayaking or paddle boarding tour in Big Sur's coastal waters.

Alternatively, go horseback riding in the beautiful wilderness.

Visit the Henry Miller Memorial Library, a cultural center with a bookstore and lovely garden.

Dine at Nepenthe, a renowned restaurant with panoramic views of the coastline.

Day 5: tourPfeiffer Big Sur State Park

Spend a full day hiking in Pfeiffer Big Sur State Park. Trails like the Valley View and Buzzard's Roost offer spectacular views.

Bring a picnic and enjoy lunch surrounded by the serene redwood forest.

Visit the Big Sur Lodge and take a leisurely walk around the grounds.

Day 6: Art and Culture

tourthe art galleries and studios of Big Sur, showcasing the talents of local artists.
Visit the Hawthorne Gallery, known for its contemporary art exhibitions.
Learn about the history of the area at the Big Sur Historical Society.
Enjoy dinner at one of the local restaurants and try some organic, farm-to-table cuisine.

Day 7: Departure

Before leaving Big Sur, take a scenic drive to Garrapata State Park for one last dose of rugged coastline.
Stop at Rocky Creek Bridge for some final photos.
Check out of your accommodation and start your journey back home or to your next destination.

This itinerary offers a mix of natural beauty, outdoor activities, cultural experiences, and relaxation. Be sure to check the weather and trail conditions before heading out, and make reservations where necessary, as Big Sur can get quite busy, especially during peak tourist seasons. Enjoy your trip.

Chapter Two: Getting There

Transportation Options

Big Sur Coast offers breathtaking natural beauty and numerous attractions for tourists and travelers. When it comes to transportation options, getting to and around Big Sur requires careful planning due to its rugged terrain and limited infrastructure. Here's description of transportation options for visitors:

Car Rental: Renting a car is the most flexible and popular option. You can pick up a rental vehicle at major airports like San Francisco International Airport (SFO) or Los Angeles International Airport (LAX). From there, take Highway 1 south to Big Sur. Ensure your rental car has adequate fuel, as gas stations can be sparse.

RV or Campervan Rental: For a unique experience, consider renting an RV or campervan. Big Sur has several campgrounds where you can park and enjoy the natural surroundings.

Shuttle Services: Some tour companies and shuttle services operate in the area. They offer guided tours or point-to-point transportation, which can be a convenient way to tourBig Sur without the hassle of driving.

Bicycling: For the more adventurous traveler, cycling along the Pacific Coast Highway is an option. Be prepared for challenging terrain and varying weather conditions.

Hiking: Some tourists choose to hike into Big Sur, either from nearby parks or along the renowned Pacific Crest Trail. Make sure to check trail conditions and permits in advance.

Motorcycle Rental: If you're a motorcycle enthusiast, consider renting a bike to enjoy the winding roads and stunning coastal views. Helmets are mandatory in California.

Hitchhiking: While not recommended due to safety concerns, some travelers do opt for hitchhiking. If you choose this route, exercise caution and always prioritize safety.

Carpooling and Ride-Sharing: Apps like Uber and Lyft can be used for short distances within Big Sur, but availability may be limited.

Local Tours: Joining local tours and excursions can be an excellent way to tour the region without worrying about transportation logistics. These tours often include transportation, guides, and planned stops at popular attractions.

Remember that Big Sur is known for its rugged terrain, steep cliffs, and winding roads. Drive cautiously, especially if you're not familiar with the area. Plan your transportation in advance, check road conditions, and have a backup plan in case of any unexpected delays or closures. By choosing the right transportation option, you can fully dip yourself in the stunning beauty of the Big Sur Coast.

Public Transportation

Traveling to Big Sur Coast using public transportation can be a unique and environmentally friendly experience. Getting to Big Sur via public transportation allows travelers to enjoy the journey as much as the destination. Here's how to use public transportation to reach Big Sur Coast:

Start Your Journey: Most travelers will likely begin their trip to Big Sur from San Francisco, which is a common starting point. You can take a flight or arrive at San Francisco International Airport (SFO) if you're coming from afar.

Arriving in San Francisco: Once you arrive in San Francisco, you have several options to reach Big Sur by public transportation.

Bus Services: Take a bus from San Francisco to Monterey, which is the gateway to Big Sur. The Monterey-Salinas Transit (MST) provides regular bus services between these two cities. The journey offers scenic views of the coast, and it takes approximately 2.5 to 3 hours.

From Monterey, you can catch another MST bus that will take you along Highway 1, offering breathtaking views of the coastline, and eventually reach various stops in Big Sur.

Amtrak Train: You can also opt for an Amtrak train journey. Take an Amtrak train from San Francisco to Salinas, where you can transfer to a bus that connects to Big Sur.

Traveling by Bike: For the more adventurous traveler, consider biking to Big Sur. You can rent a bicycle in San Francisco and follow the Pacific Coast Highway (Highway 1) southward. Be prepared for a challenging yet rewarding journey with stunning coastal views.

Lodging Options: Big Sur offers a range of lodging options, including campgrounds, cabins, and upscale resorts. Be sure to book your accommodations in advance, especially during peak tourist seasons.

fascinating Big Sur: Once you've arrived, public transportation options within Big Sur are limited. Consider renting a car, bike, or even using a rideshare service to tour the area more conveniently. Many of Big Sur's famous attractions, like Bixby Creek Bridge and McWay Falls, are accessible by road.

Eco-Friendly Choices: While in Big Sur, make eco-friendly choices to minimize your impact on the environment. Respect the natural beauty of the area, practice Leave No Trace principles, and support sustainable businesses.

Return Journey: To return to San Francisco, simply reverse your journey by taking a bus or train from Big Sur back to Monterey or Salinas and then connecting to transportation to San Francisco.

Traveling to Big Sur by public transportation can be an adventure in itself, allowing you to appreciate the rugged coastal beauty and reduce your carbon footprint. Be sure to check schedules and routes in advance, as they may vary depending on the time of year and availability. Enjoy your trip to one of California's most breathtaking destinations.

Airports Nearby

The Big Sur Coast offers breathtaking views of the rugged coastline and pristine wilderness. While there aren't any airports directly in Big Sur, several airports nearby provide convenient access for tourists and travelers. Here's an elaborate and detailed description of these airports:

Monterey Regional Airport (MRY):

Distance from Big Sur: Approximately 30 miles (48 kilometers) to the north.
Description: Monterey Regional Airport is the closest airport to Big Sur, making it a popular choice for travelers. It offers domestic flights, including connections to major hubs like San Francisco and Los Angeles.
Facilities: The airport features car rental services, dining options, and ground transportation to Big Sur via shuttle or rental cars.

San Jose International Airport (SJC):

Distance from Big Sur: Approximately 85 miles (137 kilometers) to the north.

Description: San Jose International Airport is a larger airport with a wide range of domestic and international flights. It's a major hub in the Bay Area, offering more flight options.

Facilities: The airport boasts numerous dining and shopping options, car rental services, and convenient highway access to Highway 1, which leads to Big Sur.

San Francisco International Airport (SFO):

Distance from Big Sur: Approximately 120 miles (193 kilometers) to the north.

Description: SFO is one of the busiest airports on the West Coast and offers extensive domestic and international flight connections. While it's farther from Big Sur, it's a popular choice for travelers planning a California trip.

Facilities: The airport offers a wide array of amenities, including shopping, dining, car rentals, and various ground transportation options.

Los Angeles International Airport (LAX):

Distance from Big Sur: Approximately 280 miles (450 kilometers) to the south.

Description: LAX is a major international gateway with connections to destinations worldwide. Travelers coming from farther afield may opt for this airport and combine their visit to Big Sur with other Southern California attractions.

Facilities: LAX provides extensive services, including car rentals, dining, and a variety of transportation options.

Travelers can choose their airport based on their origin, travel plans, and preferences. From any of these airports, renting a car is a popular option to tourthe scenic drive along Highway 1 and experience the natural beauty of Big Sur Coast. Additionally, shuttle services and public transportation are available for those who prefer not to drive.

Chapter Three: Accommodation Options

Hotels and Resorts

Here's the list list of Hotels and Resorts in Big Sur Coast that both tourists and travelers can take advantage of:

Ventana Big Sur

Location: Approximately 36.2462° N, 121.7842° W

Post Ranch Inn

Location: Approximately 36.2357° N, 121.8042° W

Big Sur River Inn

Location: Approximately 36.2663° N, 121.7882° W

Nepenthe Restaurant and Inn

Location: Approximately 36.2106° N, 121.7537° W

Ragged Point Inn and Resort

Location: Approximately 35.7326° N, 121.3242° W

Treebones Resort

Location: Approximately 35.6692° N, 121.2747° W

Ventana Campground

Location: Approximately 36.2289° N, 121.8051° W

Lucia Lodge

Location: Approximately 36.0274° N, 121.5186° W

Fernwood Resort

Location: Approximately 36.1559° N, 121.6583° W

Esalen Institute

Location: Approximately 36.1916° N, 121.3906° W

These establishments offer various accommodations, from luxurious resorts to campgrounds, providing options for travelers fascinating the stunning Big Sur Coast. Please remember to check the most up-to-date information, including reservations and availability, before planning your visit.

Campgrounds and RV Parks

Big Sur Coast is known for its dramatic landscapes and breathtaking views of the Pacific Ocean. Here are some campgrounds and RV parks in the Big Sur area, along with their names and locations:

Pfeiffer Big Sur State Park Campground

Location: 47225 CA-1, Big Sur, CA 93920
Description: This popular campground is settled among redwood trees and offers various campsites, including RV-friendly spots. It's a short drive to Pfeiffer Beach and McWay Falls.

Andrew Molera State Park Campground

Location: 47455 CA-1, Big Sur, CA 93920
Description: A rustic campground with walk-in sites, Andrew Molera State Park Campground is perfect for those seeking a more secluded camping experience. It's close to hiking trails and the Big Sur River.

Kirk Creek Campground

Location: 96700 CA-1, Big Sur, CA 93920
Description: Perched on a bluff overlooking the ocean, Kirk Creek Campground offers breathtaking

views and tent and RV sites. It's known for its stunning sunsets and proximity to Sand Dollar Beach.

Plaskett Creek Campground

Location: 69512 CA-1, Big Sur, CA 93920
Description: This campground is situated amidst coastal vegetation and has RV sites with hookups. It's near Jade Cove, where you can search for jade along the shoreline.

Ventana Campground

Location: 48123 CA-1, Big Sur, CA 93920
Description: Ventana Campground is part of the Ventana Big Sur resort and offers upscale camping experiences, including glamping tents and RV sites with full hookups. It's a luxurious option in the area.

Fernwood Resort and Campground

Location: 47200 CA-1, Big Sur, CA 93920
Description: Fernwood is a family-friendly campground and resort with a range of accommodation options, including tent sites, cabins, and RV sites. It features an on-site restaurant and general store.

Riverside Campground and Cabins

Location: 47020 CA-1, Big Sur, CA 93920
Description: This campground offers a peaceful riverside setting and a variety of camping options. It's close to attractions like Bixby Creek Bridge and Point Sur State Historic Park.

Limekiln State Park Campground

Location: 63025 CA-1, Big Sur, CA 93920
Description: Limekiln State Park Campground is situated in a lush canyon and offers hiking trails, RV sites, and access to Limekiln Beach and waterfalls.

These campgrounds and RV parks in Big Sur Coast offer a range of experiences, from rustic camping in the redwoods to more upscale accommodations with ocean views. Be sure to check availability and make reservations in advance, as Big Sur is a popular destination for tourists and travelers. Enjoy your visit to this stunning coastal paradise.

Cabins and Vacation Rentals

Cabins and vacation rentals offer unique and immersive accommodation options for tourists and travelers fascinating the stunning Big Sur Coast.

settled amidst the rugged beauty of the California coastline, these accommodations provide an intimate and authentic experience that complements the natural wonders of the area.

Cabins:

Location: Cabins in Big Sur are strategically placed to provide breathtaking views of the Pacific Ocean or the lush forests that characterize the region. You can find them perched on cliffs, tucked away in redwood groves, or situated alongside pristine creeks.

Architecture: Many cabins in Big Sur feature rustic yet pleasant architecture with wood and stone elements that blend seamlessly with the surrounding landscape. Large windows and open floor plans allow guests to connect with nature while enjoying modern comforts.

Amenities: While cabins offer a rustic feel, they are equipped with essential amenities such as fully-equipped kitchens, cozy fireplaces, and private outdoor spaces like decks or patios. Some even have hot tubs where you can soak while gazing at the starry night sky.

Privacy: Cabins in Big Sur provide a sense of seclusion and tranquility, making them perfect for romantic getaways or quiet retreats. You'll often find that your nearest neighbors are the local wildlife.

Adventure Access: Many cabins are located near hiking trails, beaches, and state parks, making them an ideal choice for outdoor enthusiasts who want easy access to the natural wonders of Big Sur.

Vacation Rentals:

Diverse Options: Vacation rentals in Big Sur offer a wide range of choices, from cozy cottages and beachfront bungalows to spacious hilltop villas. This diversity allows travelers to find accommodations that suit their preferences and group size.

Local Flair: These rentals often reflect the artistic and bohemian spirit of the Big Sur community, featuring eclectic decor, unique artwork, and a sense of local authenticity.

Kitchens and Living Spaces: Vacation rentals typically come with fully-equipped kitchens and spacious living areas, making them suitable for extended stays and family vacations.

Outdoor Spaces: Many vacation rentals boast expansive outdoor spaces, including decks, gardens, and patios, where guests can relax, dine al fresco, and soak in the incredible ocean or mountain views.

Community Interaction: Staying in a vacation rental can provide opportunities for interaction with local hosts who can offer insider tips on the best spots to tour in Big Sur, enhancing the overall travel experience.

Both cabins and vacation rentals in Big Sur allow travelers to disconnect from the hustle and bustle of everyday life and reconnect with the natural beauty of the region. Whether you prefer the cozy seclusion of a cabin or the eclectic beauty of a vacation rental, these accommodation options enhance the allure of Big Sur's majestic coastline and its awe-inspiring landscapes.

Chapter Four: Booking Tips and Recommendations

Popular Lodging Choices

When it comes to choosing lodging options for a visit to the stunning Big Sur Coast, you'll find a variety of choices that cater to different preferences and budgets. Here's a description of popular lodging choices along with booking tips and recommendations for tourists and travelers:

Luxury Resorts: Post Ranch Inn: Perched on cliffs overlooking the Pacific, this high-end resort offers luxurious treehouse-style rooms and cliffside suites. It's perfect for honeymooners and those seeking seclusion.

Ventana Big Sur: This adults-only resort offers a range of upscale accommodations, including glamping tents, suites, and villas. It's known for its spa, hot tubs, and scenic views.

Booking Tip: Reserve well in advance, especially during peak tourist seasons, to secure your spot at these exclusive resorts.

Boutique Inns:

Big Sur River Inn: settled along the Big Sur River, this historic inn offers pleasant rooms and cottages. It's a great choice for a cozy, rustic experience.

Ragged Point Inn: Located at the southern end of Big Sur, this inn provides panoramic ocean views and comfortable rooms. Their on-site restaurant is a highlight.

Booking Tip: Consider staying mid-week or during the shoulder seasons for better availability and lower rates.

Camping and Glamping:

Pfeiffer Big Sur State Park: Campers can enjoy the natural beauty of Big Sur in campsites settled among the redwoods. Reserve your campsite online through the California State Parks website.

Treebones Resort: For a unique experience, try glamping in yurts with ocean views at Treebones. Booking in advance is crucial, especially for their popular yurts.
Booking Tip: Book campsites well ahead of your trip, and check the camping regulations in the area.

Vacation Rentals: Airbnb and VRBO: Big Sur offers numerous vacation rentals, including cottages and cabins. These can be an incredible decision for families or gatherings.

Booking Tip: Read reviews carefully and communicate with hosts to ensure your chosen rental meets your needs.

Budget-Friendly Options: Big Sur Campground and Cabins: This budget-friendly option offers campgrounds and basic cabins at a more affordable rate compared to luxury resorts.

Booking Tip: Be prepared for rustic accommodations and limited amenities at budget-friendly options.

Last-Minute Booking: If you're a spontaneous traveler, consider using last-minute booking apps or websites to find deals on accommodations in the area.

Weather Considerations:

Check the weather forecast before booking, as fog and rain can affect visibility and accessibility in Big Sur.

Length of Stay: Plan your lodging based on how many days you intend to spend in the area. Big Sur has a lot to offer, so consider a multi-day stay for tourists ' beauty fully.

Remember that Big Sur is a popular destination, and accommodations can fill up quickly, especially during the summer and holidays. Booking well in advance is key to securing your preferred lodging choice and making the most of your visit to this breathtaking coastal paradise.

Off-the-Beaten-Path Accommodations

When planning a trip to the stunning Big Sur Coast, consider venturing off the beaten path and fascinating unique accommodations that offer a one-of-a-kind experience. Here's a description of some off-the-beaten-path accommodations along with booking tips and recommendations for tourists and travelers:

Treehouse Retreats: settled in the lush redwood forests of Big Sur, treehouse accommodations provide a magical and secluded experience. These cozy treetop cabins often feature rustic interiors, private decks with breathtaking views, and a chance to dip yourself in nature. **Booking Tip:** Reserve well in advance, especially during peak travel seasons.

Yurts by the Sea: For a coastal glamping adventure, consider staying in a yurt along the rugged Big Sur coastline. These round, tent-like structures offer comfortable beds, wood-burning stoves, and easy access to hiking trails and beaches.
Booking Tip: Check for yurt availability in state parks like Pfeiffer Big Sur State Park.

Cliffside Cottages: Perched on the cliffs overlooking the Pacific Ocean, cliffside cottages provide a serene escape with unparalleled ocean views. You'll have the chance to watch fascinating sunsets from your private balcony and listen to the soothing sounds of crashing waves.
Booking Tip: These accommodations often have limited availability, so plan well in advance.

Hot Springs Hideaways: Big Sur is home to natural hot springs, and some accommodations offer private soaking tubs with hot spring water. Imagine relaxing in your own secluded tub while surrounded by towering redwoods and serene wilderness.
Booking Tip: Be sure to ask about their hot spring amenities when booking.

Cozy Airstream Camps: Vintage Airstream trailers transformed into cozy campsites can be found in various locations in Big Sur. These accommodations offer a unique blend of nostalgia and comfort, perfect for those seeking a quirky experience.

Booking Tip: Look for campgrounds that offer Airstream rentals and make reservations early.

Mountain Cabins: Escape the coastal fog by staying in a mountain cabin tucked away in the Santa Lucia Mountains. These cabins offer a peaceful retreat with hiking trails right at your doorstep.

Booking Tip: Some cabins are available through vacation rental websites, so be sure to read reviews and verify amenities.

Historic Inns:

Big Sur has a rich history, and staying in a historic inn can provide a glimpse into its past. These inns often feature pleasant architecture, gardens, and a sense of nostalgia.

Booking Tip: Research the history of the inn you're interested in to fully appreciate its heritage.

Creekside Campgrounds:

Camping beside a babbling creek offers a tranquil experience. Many campgrounds in Big Sur are situated alongside these waterways, providing a soothing ambiance for nature lovers.

Booking Tip: Check the availability and specific amenities of the campgrounds in advance.

Secluded Beach Houses: For a truly private getaway, consider renting a secluded beach house along the Big Sur coast. These properties offer the ultimate in privacy, with direct access to the beach and uninterrupted ocean views.

Booking Tip: Start your search early, as these rentals are in high demand.

Local Bed and Breakfasts:

Support local businesses by staying in a pleasant bed and breakfast. You'll enjoy personalized service, home-cooked breakfasts, and insider tips from your hosts. **Booking Tip:** Reach out to the hosts to inquire about their recommendations for fascinating Big Sur.

When booking your off-the-beaten-path accommodations in Big Sur, always consider the season and plan ahead to secure your preferred lodging. Each option offers a unique experience, allowing you to dip yourself in the natural beauty and tranquility of this iconic California destination. Enjoy your journey along the breathtaking Big Sur Coast.

Chapter Five: Outdoor Activities

Hiking and Trails

Hiking and fascinating the trails along the Big Sur Coast is an unparalleled outdoor adventure for tourists and travelers seeking a breathtaking natural experience. Big Sur boasts a unique combination of awe-inspiring landscapes, diverse ecosystems, and a rich tapestry of flora and fauna. Here's an elaborate and detailed description of hiking and trails as outdoor activities in this remarkable destination:

Scenic Diversity: Big Sur's coastline stretches for approximately 90 miles along California's Highway 1, offering a diverse range of hiking experiences. From coastal trails that meander along towering cliffs overlooking the Pacific Ocean to forested paths that lead through lush redwood groves, there's a trail for every type of hiker.

Iconic Landmarks: Some of the most renowned hiking destinations include McWay Falls, an 80-foot waterfall that cascades onto a pristine beach; Bixby Creek Bridge, an architectural marvel; and Pfeiffer Beach, famous for its unique purple-hued sands. These landmarks make for fascinating stops along the hiking routes.

Wildlife Encounters: While hiking in Big Sur, visitors have the opportunity to encounter a rich array of wildlife. Keep an eye out for California condors, gray whales, sea otters, and various bird species. The region's protected ecosystems provide a safe haven for these creatures.

Breathtaking Vistas: The dramatic coastal cliffs of Big Sur offer some of the most jaw-dropping vistas in the world. Trails like the Ewoldsen Trail and the Overlook Trail provide hikers with panoramic views of the rugged coastline, rocky promontories, and the endless expanse of the Pacific Ocean.

Redwood Magic: Venturing inland, hikers can tourthe enchanting redwood forests of Big Sur. Trails like the Pfeiffer Falls Trail and the Buzzard's Roost Trail wind through towering groves of ancient redwoods, creating an otherworldly atmosphere that transports hikers to a different time.

Challenging Terrain: Big Sur's trails cater to all skill levels, from easy walks suitable for families to strenuous hikes for experienced adventurers. The terrain varies from well-maintained paths to rugged and challenging routes, ensuring there's something for everyone.

Seasonal Beauty: The beauty of Big Sur changes with the seasons. Spring brings vibrant wildflowers, summer offers clear skies and warm temperatures, fall brings a riot of colors to the forests, and winter showcases the dramatic power of the ocean with powerful waves crashing against the cliffs.

Leave No Trace: Responsible hiking and trail etiquette is crucial in preserving the pristine beauty of Big Sur. Visitors are encouraged to follow the Leave No Trace principles, respecting the environment and minimizing their impact on this fragile ecosystem.

Planning and Permits: Many trails in Big Sur require permits or reservations, especially during peak seasons. It's essential for travelers to plan ahead, check trail conditions, and obtain any necessary permits before embarking on their hikes.

Local Culture: Beyond the natural beauty, Big Sur also has a vibrant local culture, with art galleries, pleasant cafes, and a sense of bohemian spirit. fascinating the region's culture can complement the outdoor experience.

Hiking and fascinating the trails of the Big Sur Coast is an unforgettable adventure that combines breathtaking scenery, diverse ecosystems, and a deep connection to nature. Whether you're an experienced hiker or a novice explorer, the beauty and tranquility of Big Sur's landscapes are sure to leave an indelible mark on your travel memories.

Beaches and Water Activities

Big Sur Coast offers an attractive paradise for tourists and travelers seeking outdoor activities, especially when it comes to beaches and water activities. Here's a description of these experiences.

Majestic Coastal Scenery: Big Sur's coastline boasts dramatic cliffs, rugged terrain, and breathtaking vistas. Its pristine beaches are framed by towering redwood forests and steep cliffs, creating a unique backdrop that attracts nature enthusiasts and photographers alike.

Pfeiffer Beach - A Hidden Treasure : One of the most iconic beaches in Big Sur is Pfeiffer Beach. Tucked away down a narrow, winding road, it offers a sense of exclusivity. The highlight is the Keyhole Rock, a natural arch where the sun's rays pierce through during sunset, creating a magical play of light.

Sand Dollar Beach - A Surfer's Haven: For those inclined towards surfing, Sand Dollar Beach is a favorite spot. Its long stretches of golden sands are complemented by consistently good waves, making it a surfer's haven. Even if you're not a surfer, it's a great spot to watch skilled surfers ride the waves.

Julia Pfeiffer Burns State Park: This state park is a must-visit for travelers seeking a blend of beach and nature. Here, you can take a short hike down McWay Falls Trail to witness McWay Falls, a stunning 80-foot waterfall that cascades directly onto the sandy shore. The view is truly fascinating .

Bixby Creek Bridge - Scenic Overlook: While not a beach, Bixby Creek Bridge offers a fantastic vantage point for ocean enthusiasts. Standing on this iconic bridge, you'll be treated to sweeping panoramic views of the coastline and the Pacific Ocean. It's a perfect spot for whale watching during migration seasons.

Kayaking and Paddleboarding: fascinating Big Sur's rugged coastline by kayak or paddleboard is an adventurous water activity. Rent equipment in nearby towns, and you can paddle through sea caves, kelp forests, and spot sea otters and seals in their natural habitat.

Scuba Diving and Snorkeling: For those who want to tour beneath the surface, Big Sur offers unique scuba diving and snorkeling opportunities. Divers can discover vibrant kelp forests and a diverse range of marine life, while snorkelers can enjoy clear waters and rocky coves.

Wildlife Encounters: Water activities along Big Sur's coast often provide the chance to encounter local wildlife. Keep an eye out for dolphins, sea lions, and even migrating whales, which can be spotted from various points along the shoreline.

Big Sur Coast is a coastal paradise where beaches and water activities provide an opportunity to dip yourself in the natural beauty of the region. Whether you're a beachcomber, surfer, hiker, or wildlife enthusiast, this iconic stretch of California's coastline promises unforgettable outdoor experiences for tourists and travelers.

Wildlife Viewing

Wildlife viewing in the stunning Big Sur Coast offers tourists and travelers a fascinating and immersive outdoor experience.. This region boasts a diverse ecosystem that beckons nature enthusiasts and wildlife aficionados alike.

Scenic Beauty: As you embark on your wildlife viewing adventure in Big Sur, you'll be treated to breathtaking vistas of towering cliffs, pristine beaches, and lush forests. The dramatic backdrop of the Santa Lucia Mountains provides a stunning setting for your outdoor excursion.

Rich Biodiversity: Big Sur is home to an incredible variety of wildlife, both on land and in the Pacific Ocean. From gray whales and sea otters frolicking in the kelp forests to peregrine falcons soaring overhead, the region's biodiversity is awe-inspiring.

Iconic Species: Among the charismatic species you may encounter are California condors, a critically endangered bird species that has been successfully reintroduced into the area. Observing these majestic birds with their distinctive white markings is a true privilege.

Marine Life: Don't forget to tour the tide pools along the coast, where you can discover an array of fascinating marine life, including sea anemones, starfish, and hermit crabs. Binoculars or spotting scopes can enhance your marine wildlife viewing experience.

Whale Watching: Big Sur is a hotspot for whale watching, especially during the annual gray whale migration. From December through April, these enormous marine mammals can often be spotted breaching and spouting offshore, making for an unforgettable spectacle.

Birdwatching: With over 400 bird species recorded in the region, Big Sur is a birdwatcher's paradise. Bring your binoculars and look out for Western bluebirds, California quail, and numerous raptors soaring above the cliffs.

Ethical Viewing: Responsible wildlife viewing is crucial. Keep a respectful distance from animals, avoid disturbing their natural behavior, and never feed them. This ensures the safety of both wildlife and visitors.

Guided Tours: To enhance your wildlife viewing experience, consider joining guided tours led by knowledgeable naturalists. They can provide insights into the local ecosystem, animal behavior, and conservation efforts.

Hiking Trails: Many wildlife viewing opportunities can be found along Big Sur's extensive network of hiking trails. These trails wind through diverse habitats, offering encounters with flora and fauna at every turn.

Conservation Efforts: Big Sur is not only a haven for wildlife enthusiasts but also a region deeply committed to conservation. Learn about the ongoing efforts to protect this natural treasure and how you can contribute to preserving its beauty for future generations.

Wildlife viewing in Big Sur Coast is an immersive and enriching outdoor activity that allows tourists and travelers to connect with the natural world in a breathtakingly beautiful setting. Whether you're captivated by soaring condors, playful sea otters, or the majesty of the Pacific Ocean, Big Sur promises an unforgettable adventure for those who seek to tourists untamed wilderness.

Chapter Six: Cultural and Historical Sites

Museums

Museums along the Big Sur Coast offer an enriching and immersive experience for tourists and travelers seeking to tour the region's rich cultural and historical heritage. These museums provide a unique opportunity to delve into the past and connect with the local culture.

Big Sur Historical Society Museum: Located in the heart of Big Sur Village, this museum serves as a treasure trove of the region's history. Visitors can trace the origins of Big Sur, from its indigenous people through the Spanish colonial period to the present day. The exhibits include artifacts, photographs, and interactive displays that showcase the evolution of this coastal paradise.

Henry Miller Memorial Library: Although not a traditional museum, this literary and cultural center pays homage to the famous American author, Henry Miller, who lived in Big Sur. The library hosts exhibitions, events, and workshops that celebrate Miller's work and the artistic spirit of the area. Its serene garden setting, surrounded by redwoods, is an experience in itself.

Pacific House Museum: Located in Monterey, just north of Big Sur, this museum offers a glimpse into the maritime history of the region. It features displays of shipwrecks, early navigation tools, and the cultural significance of the sea to the local communities. The museum provides a broader context for understanding Big Sur's coastal heritage.

Point Sur State Historic Park and Lighthouse: Although not a museum in the traditional sense, this site is an iconic historical landmark. Tourists can tourthe fully restored lighthouse, keeper's house, and other structures while learning about their role in guiding ships along the treacherous coast. Guided tours shed light on the fascinating history of this place.

Ventana Wildlife Society Discovery Center: This unique museum focuses on the conservation efforts to protect the California condor, a critically endangered species. Visitors can learn about the successful reintroduction program and the role of Big Sur's rugged landscape in preserving this majestic bird.

Art Galleries: While not museums per se, Big Sur is also home to several art galleries that showcase the work of local artists, many of whom draw inspiration from the area's natural beauty. These galleries often host exhibitions that blend art and culture, providing visitors with a creative perspective on Big Sur.

Museums along the Big Sur Coast offer a fascinating blend of history, culture, and natural beauty. They serve as windows into the past, shedding light on the diverse heritage of this rugged coastal region. Whether fascinating the rich history of Big Sur or admiring the works of local artists, these cultural sites add depth and meaning to the traveler's journey along this breathtaking stretch of California coastline.

Art Galleries

Art Galleries along the Big Sur Coast offer a unique blend of cultural and historical significance, making them fascinating destinations for tourists and travelers. These galleries serve as more than just spaces to admire art; they are windows into the area's rich heritage and creative spirit.

Stunning Scenery: Big Sur's dramatic landscapes provide an attractive backdrop to these art galleries.

The rugged cliffs, towering redwoods, and panoramic ocean views create an ambiance that inspires artists and enchants visitors. The galleries themselves often incorporate the natural surroundings into their designs, blending art and nature seamlessly.

Local Artistic Expression: Many of the artworks on display are crafted by local artists who draw inspiration from the region's unique environment. These galleries showcase a diverse range of artistic styles, from traditional paintings and sculptures to contemporary and experimental installations. Each piece reflects the artist's connection to the landscape and culture of Big Sur.

Historical Significance: Some art galleries in Big Sur have historical roots, dating back to the mid-20th century when the region became a haven for artists and writers. Iconic figures like Henry Miller and Ansel Adams were drawn to Big Sur's rugged allure, and their legacy is preserved in these spaces. Visiting these galleries provides a glimpse into the area's artistic history.

Cultural Insights: Art galleries also serve as cultural hubs, hosting events, exhibitions, and workshops that engage both locals and visitors. These events often celebrate the region's indigenous heritage, as well as its artistic and literary traditions. It's an opportunity for tourists to dip themselves in the cultural tapestry of Big Sur.

Preservation of Nature: Environmental awareness is a recurring theme in Big Sur's art scene. Many galleries use their platform to advocate for the preservation of the region's pristine landscapes and wildlife. Some even collaborate with conservation organizations to raise awareness and funds for environmental causes.

Community Engagement: Art galleries in Big Sur are often deeply connected to the local community. They support emerging artists, provide spaces for artistic expression, and contribute to the economic vitality of the area. Visitors have the chance to engage with artists and gain insights into the creative process.

Souvenirs and Collectibles: For travelers, these galleries offer a unique opportunity to acquire one-of-a-kind souvenirs and artworks that encapsulate the essence of Big Sur. Whether it's a painting of a coastal sunset or a sculpture inspired by the redwood forests, these pieces carry a part of Big Sur's magic.

Art galleries along the Big Sur Coast are not just places to view and purchase art; they are cultural and historical landmarks that encapsulate the spirit of this awe-inspiring region. They invite tourists and travelers to connect with the natural beauty, artistic heritage, and vibrant culture of Big Sur, leaving them with indelible memories and a deeper appreciation for this coastal paradise.

Historic Landmarks

Big Sur Coast in California is renowned for its breathtaking natural beauty and historic landmarks. Here are 15 historic landmarks, along with their names and geotag information, that serve as cultural and historical sites for tourists and travelers:

Bixby Creek Bridge

Geotag: 36.3689° N, 121.9019° W
Description: Iconic bridge known for its stunning architecture and panoramic views of the rugged coastline.

Point Sur Lighthouse

Geotag: 36.3077° N, 121.9017° W

Description: A historic lighthouse perched on a volcanic rock, offering guided tours and maritime history insights.

Julia Pfeiffer Burns State Park

Geotag: 36.1595° N, 121.6680° W
Description: Home to McWay Falls and an 80-foot waterfall that cascades onto the beach, surrounded by redwoods.

Pfeiffer Big Sur State Park

Geotag: 36.2620° N, 121.7976° W
Description: A redwood-filled park with numerous hiking trails and the Big Sur River winding through.

Boronda Adobe History Center

Geotag: 36.5737° N, 121.8364° W
Description: A preserved adobe house showcasing the history of early settlers in the region.

Big Sur River Inn

Geotag: 36.2650° N, 121.7901° W
Description: A historic inn with a restaurant, offering a rustic atmosphere and beautiful river views.

Henry Miller Memorial Library

Geotag: 36.2667° N, 121.7910° W
Description: A cultural center and bookstore dedicated to the legacy of writer Henry Miller.

Ragged Point Inn and Resort

Geotag: 35.7335° N, 121.3314° W
Description: A scenic viewpoint and inn perched on cliffs overlooking the Pacific Ocean.

Nepenthe Restaurant

Geotag: 36.2160° N, 121.7531° W
Description: A historic restaurant with incredible coastal views, known for its bohemian atmosphere.

Partington Cove

Geotag: 36.1700° N, 121.6744° W
Description: A hidden cove with a tunnel leading to a rocky beach, once used for shipping redwood logs.

Piedras Blancas Light Station

Geotag: 35.6627° N, 121.2571° W

Description: A historic lighthouse and wildlife viewing area, famous for elephant seal sightings.

Mission San Antonio de Padua

Geotag: 36.0040° N, 121.3240° W
Description: A Spanish mission dating back to 1771, featuring a beautiful chapel and gardens.

Garrapata State Park

Geotag: 36.4714° N, 121.9335° W
Description: A coastal park with rugged terrain, hiking trails, and spectacular ocean vistas.

Palo Colorado Canyon

Geotag: 36.2328° N, 121.7603° W
Description: A historic canyon known for its redwoods, hiking, and serene natural beauty.

Rocky Creek Bridge

Geotag: 36.3413° N, 121.8967° W
Description: An attractive bridge offering stunning views of the rugged coastline and the Pacific Ocean.

These landmarks showcase the rich history and natural wonders of Big Sur Coast, making it a must-visit destination for travelers and history enthusiasts alike.

Chapter Seven: Dining and Food

Restaurants and Cafes

Big sur Coast has stunning restaurants and cafes for tourists and travelers delight. Please note that specific details like hours of operation and menu offerings may change, so it's a good idea to check with the establishments or
online resources for the most up-to-date information.

Nepenthe

Description: Perched on a cliff with breathtaking ocean views, Nepenthe offers a relaxed atmosphere and a diverse menu featuring burgers, seafood, and salads.

Geotag: Latitude 36.1801° N, Longitude 121.7422° W

Sierra Mar at Post Ranch Inn

Description: Sierra Mar is an upscale restaurant known for its exquisite fine dining experience, offering a seasonal menu with locally sourced ingredients.

Geotag: Latitude 36.2357° N, Longitude 121.8122° W

Deetjen's Big Sur Inn

Description: Deetjen's is a historic inn with a cozy dining room serving hearty, homestyle dishes in a pleasant, rustic setting.
Geotag: Latitude 36.2054° N, Longitude 121.6111° W

Big Sur River Inn

Description: Located by the Big Sur River, this restaurant provides a tranquil dining experience with outdoor seating, serving American classics and a selection of local wines.
Geotag: Latitude 36.2651° N, Longitude 121.8061° W

Café Kevah

Description: settled in the gardens of Nepenthe, Café Kevah offers a more casual dining option with salads, sandwiches, and stunning vistas.
Geotag: Latitude 36.1798° N, Longitude 121.7422° W

Ragged Point Inn Restaurant

Description: Enjoy coastal views from this clifftop restaurant, featuring seafood and American cuisine, perfect for a stop along Highway 1.
Geotag: Latitude 35.7329° N, Longitude 121.3346° W

Lucia Restaurant & Bar

Description: Located at the Bernardus Lodge & Spa, Lucia offers a farm-to-table experience with a menu highlighting fresh, local ingredients.
Geotag: Latitude 36.5116° N, Longitude 121.7594° W

The Big Sur Bakery

Description: A pleasant bakery and café known for its artisanal bread, pastries, and delicious brunch options.
Geotag: Latitude 36.2547° N, Longitude 121.7844° W

Coast Café at Treebones Resort

Description: Enjoy casual dining in a yurt with ocean views, serving a menu featuring Asian and American fusion dishes.
Geotag: Latitude 35.6703° N, Longitude 121.2539° W

Big Sur Taphouse

Description: A local favorite, this taphouse offers craft beers, pub fare, and a relaxed atmosphere.
Geotag: Latitude 36.2686° N, Longitude 121.8203° W

Ventana Big Sur

Description: Ventana's restaurant offers a refined dining experience with a focus on sustainability and local ingredients, complemented by panoramic ocean views.
Geotag: Latitude 36.2326° N, Longitude 121.8008° W

Café San Simeon

Description: Located just south of Big Sur, this café offers Mexican cuisine with a scenic patio overlooking San Simeon Bay.
Geotag: Latitude 35.6411° N, Longitude 121.1879° W

The Sur House

Description: Located at Ventana Big Sur, The Sur House serves contemporary American cuisine in an elegant setting with ocean vistas.
Geotag: Latitude 36.2327° N, Longitude 121.8006° W

Ragged Point Cliffside Café

Description: This café is perfect for a quick bite with panoramic ocean views, serving sandwiches, salads, and ice cream.
Geotag: Latitude 35.7333° N, Longitude 121.3338° W

Ripplewood Resort Restaurant

Description: A family-friendly spot known for its hearty breakfasts and burgers, settled in the redwoods of Big Sur.
Geotag: Latitude 36.2747° N, Longitude 121.8353° W

These restaurants and cafes offer diverse dining experiences amidst the stunning beauty of the Big Sur Coast, making them perfect stops for tourists and travelers. Remember to check their websites or contact them directly for the most current information.

Local Cuisine

Local cuisine along the Big Sur Coast is a culinary journey that offers tourists and travelers a delightful fusion of flavors and experiences. This region boasts a unique gastronomic identity that reflects its proximity to the Pacific Ocean, lush forests, and fertile farmland. Here's description of local cuisine in Big Sur:

Seafood Extravaganza: Big Sur's location along the Pacific Ocean ensures a steady supply of fresh seafood. Tourists can savor dishes featuring locally caught treasures like Dungeness crab, abalone, salmon, and various species of rockfish. Must-try specialties include creamy clam chowder, grilled lobster tails, and smoked albacore.

Farm-to-Table Excellence: The fertile soils of Big Sur's hinterland give rise to an abundance of farm-fresh produce. Travelers can relish dishes made with organic, locally sourced vegetables, fruits, and herbs. Expect vibrant salads, artisanal cheeses, and creative vegetarian options showcasing the region's agricultural prowess.

Fusion of Culinary Styles: Big Sur's cuisine combines diverse culinary traditions, resulting in a delightful fusion of flavors. Visitors can enjoy

Mexican-inspired dishes with a coastal twist, such as seafood tacos with tangy lime crema or smoked fish tostadas topped with avocado salsa.

Coastal Grill and Barbecue: The scent of wood-fired grills and barbecue smokers wafts through the air in Big Sur. Tourists can indulge in succulent grilled meats, including tri-tip steak, ribs, and pork shoulder, often paired with zesty barbecue sauces and served alongside classic sides like coleslaw and baked beans.

Artisanal Bakeries: Local bakeries offer a mouthwatering array of artisanal bread, pastries, and desserts. Travelers can enjoy crusty sourdough bread, flaky croissants, and decadent pies made with seasonal fruits, all baked to perfection.

Wine and Craft Beer: To complement the exquisite cuisine, Big Sur offers an impressive selection of wines from nearby vineyards and craft beers from local breweries. Tourists can sip on Pinot Noir and Chardonnay while gazing at the ocean or savor IPAs and stouts infused with regional flavors.

Rustic Ambiance: Many dining establishments in Big Sur embrace a rustic and laid-back atmosphere, where tourists can dine under the towering redwoods, overlooking dramatic cliffs, or next to cozy fireplaces. The scenic surroundings enhance the overall dining experience.

Sustainability and Eco-consciousness: Big Sur places a strong emphasis on sustainability and eco-conscious practices. Many restaurants use organic ingredients, reduce waste, and support local farmers and fishermen, ensuring that visitors can indulge guilt-free.

Dining along the Big Sur Coast offers travelers a fascinating journey through the region's rich culinary tapestry. From ocean-fresh seafood to farm-to-table delicacies, this destination delights the senses with its diverse and flavorful cuisine, all set against a backdrop of breathtaking natural beauty.

Farmers' Markets

Farmers' markets along the Big Sur Coast offer a truly unique and enriching dining experience for tourists and travelers seeking a taste of the region's local flavors. These markets blend the natural beauty of the area with the vibrant culinary culture, creating an unforgettable food adventure.

Setting and Atmosphere: As you approach these farmers' markets, the scent of fresh ocean air mingles with the aroma of ripe fruits and vegetables, creating an inviting atmosphere. Set against the backdrop of the majestic Pacific Ocean and towering redwood forests, the markets provide an attractive and serene setting for dining.

Local Produce: One of the highlights of dining at Big Sur Coast farmers' markets is the access to an abundance of fresh, locally sourced produce. Farmers and artisans from the surrounding communities come together to showcase the region's agricultural bounty. Visitors can savor freshly harvested fruits, such as juicy strawberries, crisp apples, and luscious peaches. Vegetables, including heirloom tomatoes, organic greens, and sweet corn, are also in abundance. These ingredients form the foundation of many dishes prepared on-site.

Artisanal Foods: In addition to fresh produce, these markets are a treasure trove of artisanal food products. Visitors can sample and purchase a variety of gourmet items like handcrafted cheeses, small-batch jams, artisan bread, and locally produced olive oils. These products offer a taste of the region's culinary craftsmanship and make for excellent souvenirs to take home.

Local Cuisine: One of the key attractions for tourists is the opportunity to savor Big Sur's unique cuisine. At the farmers' markets, you'll find a diverse range of food vendors offering dishes that incorporate local ingredients. Seafood lovers can indulge in freshly caught fish and seafood, including grilled oysters, clam chowder, and fish tacos. For those seeking a taste of California's farm-to-table movement, there are farm-fresh salads, wood-fired pizzas, and organic food stalls.

Live Music and Entertainment: Many farmers' markets in Big Sur Coast offer live music and entertainment, creating a lively and enjoyable atmosphere. This adds to the overall experience, making it not just about food but also a cultural and social event where visitors can connect with the local community.

Community Engagement: Interacting with the passionate farmers and artisans is a key part of the experience. Tourists and travelers can learn about the history and stories behind the products, fostering a deeper connection to the region's culture.

Scenic Picnicking: Farmers' markets often provide scenic spots for picnicking. Visitors can purchase their favorite items, set up a picnic with ocean or forest views, and relish a meal in nature's embrace.

Sustainability and Eco-Friendly Practices: These markets often emphasize sustainability and eco-friendly practices, aligning with the conservation-minded ethos of Big Sur. This commitment to environmental responsibility enhances the overall experience for conscious travelers.

In conclusion, dining at farmers' markets along the Big Sur Coast offers tourists and travelers an opportunity to dip themselves in the region's natural beauty, taste its bountiful produce, and engage with its vibrant culinary culture. It's a sensory journey that not only satisfies the palate but also deepens one's connection to this enchanting coastal paradise.

Chapter Eight: fascinating Big Sur

Pfeiffer Big Sur State Park

Pfeiffer Big Sur State Park is a fascinating beauty to behold settled within the iconic Big Sur Coast of California, making it an ideal destination for tourists and travelers seeking an immersive and awe-inspiring experience. Situated approximately 26 miles south of Monterey, this state park spans over 1,000 acres and offers a diverse range of activities and sights to explore.

Towering Redwoods: As you enter the park, you'll be greeted by the majestic coastal redwoods that define this region. These towering giants, some of which are centuries old, create a mystical atmosphere as their dense canopies filter the sunlight, casting enchanting shadows on the forest floor.

Hiking Trails: Pfeiffer Big Sur State Park boasts an extensive network of hiking trails that cater to all skill levels. The Buzzard's Roost Trail is a popular choice, leading to a panoramic viewpoint overlooking the rugged coastline. The Pfeiffer Falls Trail takes you through a lush forest to an attractive waterfall. Meanwhile, the Valley View Trail offers a tranquil stroll along the Big Sur River.

Campgrounds: For those seeking an authentic outdoor experience, the park offers several campgrounds. Pfeiffer Big Sur Campground provides a serene setting beneath the towering trees, while Ventana Campground offers a more rustic experience along the banks of the Big Sur River.

Wildlife Watching: Keep an eye out for diverse wildlife that call the park home. Deer, raccoons, bobcats, and even the occasional California condor can be spotted here. People who love to watch birds will be elated to see the different types of birds within the area.

Scenic Drives: While fascinating Big Sur Coast, the drive along California Highway 1, which passes through the park, is an attraction in itself. The highway offers breathtaking vistas of rugged cliffs, crashing waves, and the shimmering Pacific Ocean.

McWay Falls: A short drive south of the park lies McWay Falls, one of the most iconic sights along the Big Sur Coast. This 80-foot waterfall cascades directly onto a pristine beach, creating a postcard-perfect view.

Interpretive Center: The Big Sur Discovery Center within the park provides valuable insights into the region's ecology, history, and conservation efforts. It's a great place to learn more about the park's unique features.

Photography Opportunities: Pfeiffer Big Sur State Park is a photographer's paradise, offering countless opportunities to capture the natural beauty of the area. Sunrise and sunset provide magical lighting for stunning shots.

Starry Nights: With minimal light pollution, the park is an excellent spot for stargazing. On clear nights, the sky comes alive with a dazzling display of stars.

Picnicking: Several picnic areas are scattered throughout the park, providing a scenic backdrop for a leisurely outdoor meal with family and friends.

Pfeiffer Big Sur State Park is a fascinating haven of natural beauty and outdoor adventure, offering a multitude of activities for tourists and travelers eager to dip themselves in the breathtaking landscapes of California's Big Sur Coast. Whether you're an avid hiker, a nature enthusiast, or simply seeking a tranquil escape, this park promises an unforgettable experience.

Julia Pfeiffer Burns State Park

Julia Pfeiffer Burns State Park is a stunning coastal treasure located in the heart of California's Big Sur region. This park offers travelers an exquisite blend of natural beauty and outdoor adventure. Here's a description, along with geotag information, to help tourists and travelers tour this remarkable destination:

Location:

Geotag: Latitude 36.1563° N, Longitude 121.6736° W

Address: Julia Pfeiffer Burns State Park, Big Sur, California, 93920, USA

Julia Pfeiffer Burns State Park covers approximately 3,762 acres of coastal wilderness and is renowned for its breathtaking vistas, lush forests, and the iconic McWay Falls, which cascades directly onto a pristine sandy cove. The park is a must-visit for nature enthusiasts, hikers, photographers, and anyone seeking an authentic coastal California experience.

Key Attractions:

McWay Falls: The centerpiece of the park, McWay Falls, is an 80-foot waterfall that drops from a granite cliff into a turquoise cove. The view is accessible via a short trail and provides an ideal photo opportunity.

Overlook Trail: This easy 0.64-mile trail offers panoramic views of the coastline, including McWay Falls. It's a perfect introduction to the park's beauty.

Ewoldsen Trail: For more adventurous hikers, the Ewoldsen Trail is a 4.5-mile loop through redwood and oak forests, providing stunning vistas of the Pacific Ocean and rugged cliffs.

Partington Cove: Located just south of the main park entrance, Partington Cove offers a unique experience. Hike a short trail to a hidden cove with an old boat hoist, where you can tour sea caves and tide pools.

Waterfall House Ruins: tour the remains of the Waterfall House, a historic home perched above McWay Falls, offering insight into the area's history.

Visitor Information:

Hours: Julia Pfeiffer Burns State Park is typically open from sunrise to sunset.

Parking: Limited parking is available near the park entrance. Ensure to be there early to have a convenient spot, moreover when it is during peak tourist period. Facilities: The park has restrooms and picnic areas for visitors.

Travel Tips:

Dress in layers, as coastal weather can change rapidly.
Stay on designated trails to protect the fragile ecosystems.
Respect all posted signs and regulations.
Be prepared with food, water, and sunscreen, as amenities are limited.

Julia Pfeiffer Burns State Park is a place where the rugged California coastline meets the tranquility of ancient redwood forests. It's a destination that promises awe-inspiring views, memorable hikes, and a deep connection to the natural wonders of Big Sur. Whether you're an adventure seeker or a nature lover, this park is a true jewel of the Pacific Coast, offering an unforgettable experience for travelers and tourists alike.

Backpacking Trails

Fascinating the Big Sur Coast through backpacking trails offers an unparalleled adventure for tourists and travelers seeking to dip themselves in the breathtaking natural beauty of this iconic region. Here's an elaborate and detailed description of some of the most enticing backpacking trails in Big Sur:

McWay Falls Overlook Trail: This short and easily accessible trail provides a quick taste of Big Sur's beauty. Hikers will be greeted by the fascinating McWay Falls, a stunning 80-foot waterfall that cascades onto a secluded beach, creating a postcard-worthy view.

Ewoldsen Trail: For those looking for a moderate day hike, the Ewoldsen Trail is a fantastic choice. It winds through redwood forests, offering glimpses of the rugged coastline and the opportunity to tourlush canyons.

Pfeiffer Big Sur State Park Trails: This state park boasts a network of trails suitable for various skill levels. The Buzzard's Roost Trail and Valley View Trail are standout options, providing panoramic views of the Santa Lucia Mountains and the Pacific Ocean.

Julia Pfeiffer Burns State Park: Home to the iconic McWay Falls, this park offers more than just a single viewpoint. The Canyon Trail leads to a ridge with sweeping coastal vistas, while the Waters Trail allows you to venture closer to McWay Falls, where you can feel the mist from the waterfall.

Ventana Wilderness - Sykes Hot Springs Trail: For the intrepid backpacker, the Sykes Hot Springs Trail is an adventure of a lifetime. This multi-day trek takes you deep into the Ventana Wilderness, where you'll encounter remote wilderness, stunning river crossings, and, as the name suggests, natural hot springs perfect for a soak under the stars.

Salmon Creek Trail: This challenging hike is rewarded with secluded beaches and stunning sea cliffs. It's a demanding trail that leads to the beautiful Salmon Creek Falls, where hikers can cool off in the refreshing pools.

Tanbark Trail: Offering a mix of coastal and forested scenery, the Tanbark Trail is a hidden treasure . The path leads to pristine beaches, tide pools, and tide falls, with opportunities for tidepool exploration and whale watching during migration seasons.

Cones and The Tin House: A unique and off-the-beaten-path experience, this trail takes you to an abandoned tin house perched on a cliff's edge. The rugged terrain and solitude make it an ideal choice for seasoned hikers looking for solitude.

Before embarking on any backpacking adventure in Big Sur, it's crucial to check trail conditions, obtain necessary permits, and practice Leave No Trace principles to preserve the natural beauty of this remarkable coastline. Fascinating Big Sur's backpacking trails is not just a journey through stunning landscapes; it's a chance to connect with nature on a profound level, creating memories that will last a lifetime.

Wildlife and Wilderness Tips

fascinating the Big Sur Coast offers a unique opportunity to dip yourself in stunning wilderness and observe diverse wildlife. To make the most of your journey, here are some tips:

Research and Preparation: Begin your adventure by researching the Big Sur region. Learn about its geography, weather patterns, and the types of wildlife you might encounter.

Ensure that the weather and road conditions are good before leaving. Big Sur can experience heavy rainfall and road closures during the winter.

Wildlife Awareness: Big Sur is home to a variety of wildlife, including black bears, mountain lions, bobcats, and numerous bird species. Be aware of their presence and respectful of their habitat.
Carry binoculars and a wildlife field guide to help you identify and observe animals from a safe distance.
Keep a respectful distance from wildlife and never feed them. Feeding disrupts their natural behavior and can be dangerous for both animals and humans.

Hiking and Camping: Big Sur offers numerous hiking trails and campsites. Research the available trails and campsites, and obtain any necessary permits in advance.
Practice Leave No Trace principles by packing out all your trash, staying on established trails, and camping in designated areas.

Safety First: Inform someone of your itinerary before setting out on a hike or camping trip. Sometimes the network on cell phones may fluctuate. Carry essential supplies such as water, food, a first-aid kit, and navigation tools like a map and compass.

Be cautious of poison oak, which is prevalent in the region. Be sure to know and avoid coming in contact.

Respect the Environment: Stay on marked trails to prevent soil erosion and protect delicate ecosystems.
Do not pick plants or disturb natural formations. Leave rocks, shells, and other natural objects where you find them.
Practice responsible campfire etiquette, and use established fire rings or stoves where fires are permitted.

Scenic Drives: tour the breathtaking scenery along Highway 1, which winds through Big Sur. There are plenty of pullouts and vista points for photo opportunities.
Drive cautiously along the narrow and winding roads, and watch for wildlife crossing.

Local Culture and History: Take time to learn about the cultural and historical significance of Big Sur. Visit local museums and art galleries to gain a deeper understanding of the area's heritage.

Leave No Trace: Follow the Leave No Trace principles to minimize your impact on the environment. This includes packing out all trash, using established facilities, and respecting wildlife.

Permits and Regulations: Be aware of any permits or regulations in place for hiking, camping, or fishing in the area. Abide by these rules to protect the wilderness and ensure a safe experience.

Emergency Preparedness: Have a plan for emergencies, including knowing the location of the nearest medical facilities and emergency contact numbers.

By following these tips and being mindful of the natural beauty and wildlife in Big Sur, you can have an unforgettable and responsible adventure in this remarkable coastal wilderness. Enjoy your journey.

McWay Falls

McWay Falls, a fascinating waterfall, is a must-visit destination for tourists and travelers seeking the beauty of the Pacific coastline. Here's description, along with geotag information, to enhance your exploration of McWay Falls:

McWay Falls is an iconic 80-foot waterfall that plunges gracefully onto a pristine, inaccessible beach cove, making it one of the few "tidefall" waterfalls in the United States. What sets this waterfall apart is its unique location, with the turquoise waters of the Pacific Ocean forming an idyllic backdrop. The sight of the waterfall cascading directly into the ocean against the backdrop of rocky cliffs and lush greenery is nothing short of enchanting.

The cove beneath McWay Falls is a protected area, so visitors cannot access the beach directly. However, a well-maintained viewpoint provides the perfect vantage point to admire this natural wonder. The viewpoint offers panoramic views of the waterfall, the cove, and the rugged coastline, making it an ideal spot for photography and taking in the serene beauty of Big Sur.

Geotag Information:
Coordinates: Latitude 36.1615° N, Longitude 121.6681° W
Location: McWay Falls is located approximately 37 miles south of Monterey and 15 miles north of the town of Cambria along the Pacific Coast Highway (California State Route 1).
Access: To reach the McWay Falls viewpoint, travelers can park at the Julia Pfeiffer Burns State Park parking lot. The entrance to the park is well-marked on Highway 1. From there, a short, easy hike of around 0.6 miles will lead you to the

viewpoint. Visitors of all ages will find the trail safe and well-kept.

Exploration Tips:

Timing: Visit McWay Falls during daylight hours for the best lighting conditions, as the waterfall and cove are most photogenic in the soft, golden light of sunrise or sunset.

Crowd Avoidance: To avoid crowds, consider visiting on weekdays or during the off-season (late fall or winter).

Weather Preparedness: The weather along the Big Sur Coast can be variable, so bring layers and be prepared for potential coastal fog or mist.

Camera Gear: Don't forget your camera or smartphone for capturing the stunning scenery. A wide-angle lens is great for capturing the entire waterfall and cove.

Respect Nature: Remember to respect the environment and stay on designated trails to preserve the fragile ecosystem of this area.

McWay Falls is a magical destination that encapsulates the natural beauty of the Big Sur

Coast. Whether you're an avid photographer, nature enthusiast, or simply seeking a tranquil escape, this iconic waterfall is a must-visit stop on your journey along the Pacific Coast Highway. Enjoy the awe-inspiring views and create lasting memories of this attractive slice of California's coastline.

Bixby Creek Bridge

Bixby Creek Bridge is an attractive and iconic landmark located along California's stunning Big Sur Coast, making it a must-visit destination for tourists and travelers alike. This engineering marvel not only serves as a crucial transportation link along Highway 1 but also offers breathtaking views of the rugged coastline and the Pacific Ocean.

Geotag Information:
Coordinates: 36.3714° N latitude, 121.9017° W longitude
Address: Bixby Creek Bridge, Big Sur, California, 93920, USA

Bixby Creek Bridge is renowned for its architectural beauty and its location amidst the rugged cliffs and lush coastal vegetation of Big Sur. Here's description of this remarkable bridge:

Architectural Marvel: Bixby Creek Bridge is an arched concrete bridge that spans a 714-foot gap between two towering cliffs. Its graceful, sweeping design is a testament to the engineering ingenuity of its time, and it has been capturing the hearts of visitors for decades.

Natural Beauty: The bridge provides an excellent vantage point to take in the breathtaking views of the rugged Big Sur coastline. The azure waters of the Pacific Ocean stretch out endlessly, contrasting with the rocky cliffs and the lush greenery that surrounds the area. It's a photographer's dream, especially during sunrise and sunset when the golden hues paint the scene with magical light.

Wildlife Viewing: Keep an eye out for wildlife in the area.
Seabirds, including pelicans and seagulls, often roam around the bridge, and if you're lucky, you might spot a whale breaching in the distance during migration seasons.

Accessibility: Bixby Creek Bridge is easily accessible by car via California State Route 1 (also known as the Pacific Coast Highway). There is a designated parking area on the northern side of the bridge, allowing visitors to stop and admire the view safely.

Photography Opportunities: Whether you're a professional photographer or just want to capture memories, Bixby Creek Bridge offers countless opportunities for stunning photographs. The bridge itself, with its graceful arch and rugged backdrop, makes for an iconic shot, and the changing coastal weather and lighting conditions ensure every visit is unique.

Local Lore: The bridge has its own unique history, adding to its allure. It was completed in 1932 and was once the longest concrete arch span bridge in the world. The name "Bixby" comes from Charles Henry Bixby, a pioneer in the area who played a significant role in the development of Big Sur.

Nearby Attractions: While visiting Bixby Creek Bridge, you can also tour nearby attractions in Big Sur, such as McWay Falls, Pfeiffer Big Sur State Park, and the Henry Miller Memorial Library.

Bixby Creek Bridge is not just a transportation link; it's a fascinating destination in itself. It's a place where visitors can dip themselves in the natural beauty of Big Sur while appreciating the artistry of human engineering. Whether you're a nature enthusiast, a history buff, or simply in search of an awe-inspiring view, Bixby Creek Bridge should be on your travel itinerary when fascinating the Big Sur Coast.

Elephant Seal Rookery

The Elephant Seal Rookery draws tourists and travelers from around the world. Located at Piedras Blancas, approximately 5 miles north of San Simeon, California, this geotagged destination offers a unique and awe-inspiring wildlife experience.

The Elephant Seal Rookery is settled within a pristine coastal landscape characterized by rugged cliffs, dramatic ocean vistas, and the soothing sounds of crashing waves. This rookery is home to thousands of northern elephant seals, making it one of the largest and most accessible colonies in the world.

Geotag Information:

Location: Piedras Blancas, San Simeon, California, USA
Coordinates: 35.6671° N, 121.2597° W
Highlights and Activities:

Elephant Seal Viewing: Visitors can observe these massive marine mammals in their natural habitat.

The best times for viewing are during the breeding and molting seasons, which typically occur from December through March and late spring.

Educational Signage: Informative signs along the boardwalk provide valuable insights into the life cycle and behavior of elephant seals, as well as the conservation efforts in place to protect them.

Scenic Overlook: A designated viewing area offers breathtaking panoramic views of the rugged coastline and the Pacific Ocean. It's an ideal spot for photography and taking in the natural beauty of Big Sur.

Visitor Center: Nearby, there's a visitor center where tourists can learn more about elephant seals through interactive exhibits, videos, and knowledgeable staff.

Guided Tours: Knowledgeable naturalists often lead guided tours, providing in-depth information about the seals and the surrounding ecosystem.

Picnic Area: There's a convenient picnic area for visitors to enjoy a meal while taking in the stunning coastal scenery.

Conservation Efforts: The Elephant Seal Rookery plays a vital role in elephant seal conservation. Visitors can learn about ongoing efforts to protect these incredible animals and their habitats.

Travel Tips: Dress in layers, as coastal weather can be unpredictable.
Bring binoculars and a camera with a zoom lens for better seal watching and photography.
Stay on designated paths and respect the viewing guidelines to minimize disturbance to the seals.

The Elephant Seal Rookery is just one of the many natural wonders along the Big Sur Coast. Travelers can continue their journey to tour the iconic Bixby Creek Bridge, McWay Falls, Julia Pfeiffer Burns State Park, and countless other scenic spots that make this stretch of California's coastline a must-visit destination for nature enthusiasts and adventure seekers.

Ventana Wilderness

Ventana Wilderness offers an unparalleled opportunity for tourists and travelers to dip themselves in the breathtaking beauty of the Big Sur Coast. This pristine wilderness, encompassing over 240,000 acres within the Los Padres National Forest in California, promises an unforgettable adventure.

Scenic Beauty: The Ventana Wilderness is a haven for nature enthusiasts. Towering redwood and coniferous forests, juxtaposed against rugged coastal cliffs and the azure Pacific Ocean, create a landscape that's nothing short of spectacular. The region's rugged terrain and diverse ecosystems provide endless opportunities for exploration.

Hiking Trails: Ventana Wilderness boasts an extensive network of hiking trails, catering to all levels of outdoor enthusiasts. For a challenging trek, the Ventana Double Cone Trail leads to the breathtaking Double Cone Peak, offering panoramic vistas of the entire wilderness. Those seeking a more leisurely hike can tourthe scenic Pine Ridge Trail or the coastal views along the Cruickshank Trail.

Wildlife Viewing: Keep an eye out for the diverse wildlife that calls Ventana Wilderness home. You might encounter black bears, bobcats, foxes, and a variety of bird species. The wilderness is also known for its California condor population, a rare sight that thrills birdwatchers.

Camping: Camping in Ventana Wilderness is a true escape from civilization. Several campgrounds, including Bottcher's Gap and Pico Blanco, provide a rustic experience. However, backcountry camping is the real draw, allowing visitors to dip themselves in the wilderness. Permits are required and can be obtained from the Los Padres National Forest office.

Hot Springs: The region is famous for its natural hot springs, such as Sykes Hot Springs. A hike along the Pine Ridge Trail leads to these rejuvenating pools, settled amidst the wilderness. Soaking in these geothermal wonders under the stars is a magical experience.

Leave No Trace: Ventana Wilderness emphasizes responsible tourism. Visitors are encouraged to follow the "Leave No Trace" principles, ensuring the preservation of this pristine environment for future generations.

Weather Considerations: Be prepared for the variable coastal climate. Coastal fog can roll in unexpectedly, and conditions can change rapidly. It's essential to dress in layers, carry adequate supplies, and check the weather forecast before embarking on any adventure.

Permits and Regulations: Always check for current permit requirements and regulations, as they may change over time. Stay informed to ensure a safe and responsible visit.

Ventana Wilderness is a natural wonderland, offering a chance to disconnect from the modern world and reconnect with the majesty of nature. Whether you're an avid hiker, wildlife enthusiast, or simply seeking solace in a stunning coastal landscape, this wilderness beckons with its unparalleled beauty and untamed spirit. It's a destination that invites you to explore, dream, and discover the essence of Big Sur's coastal allure.

Chapter Nine: Nearby Attractions

Monterey and Carmel-by-the-Sea

Monterey and Carmel-by-the-Ocean are two beautiful seaside towns situated along the dazzling Big Sur Coast in California, offering a rich embroidery of normal magnificence, social attractions, and culinary pleasures for tourists and travelers alike.

Monterey:

Natural Beauty: Monterey boasts a ruggedly beautiful coastline with dramatic cliffs and pristine beaches. One of its most iconic natural attractions is the Monterey Bay Aquarium, renowned for its fascinating marine exhibits, including a fascinating kelp forest and a variety of sea creatures. The scenic 17-Mile Drive takes visitors through Pebble Beach, offering breathtaking vistas of the Pacific Ocean and the famous Lone Cypress Tree.

Wildlife: Whale-watching is a popular activity here, as the waters off Monterey Bay are a haven for humpback whales, blue whales, and orcas. Visitors can also spot sea otters, seals, and sea lions basking on the shores or playing in the kelp forests.

History and Culture: Cannery Row, once the center of the sardine-packing industry, is now a vibrant waterfront district filled with shops, restaurants, and historical sites. The city also boasts historic adobes, like the Custom House and Colton Hall, where California's first constitution was drafted.

Carmel-by-the-Sea:

Quaint Beauty: Just a short drive from Monterey, Carmel-by-the-Sea is an attractive village that exudes old-world beauty. The town is famous for its fairytale-like architecture, with pleasant cottages, cobblestone streets, and storybook-style buildings. The white-sand Carmel Beach is a serene spot for relaxation and scenic walks.

Art and Galleries: Carmel is an artistic hub, home to numerous galleries and art studios. It was once home to famous photographer Edward Weston and has a strong artistic heritage. The Carmel Art Association and the annual Carmel Art Festival celebrate the town's artistic spirit.

Shopping and Dining: The town's Ocean Avenue is lined with upscale boutiques, art galleries, and gourmet restaurants. It's a fantastic place for shopping for unique souvenirs and enjoying fine dining experiences. Carmel's culinary scene is diverse, offering everything from fresh seafood to international cuisine.

Wine Tasting: The nearby Carmel Valley is a hidden Treasure for wine enthusiasts. It's home to numerous wineries and tasting rooms, making it a great destination for wine tasting and vineyard tours.

Monterey and Carmel-by-the-Sea provide a fascinating blend of natural wonders, cultural richness, and a tranquil ambiance, making them an irresistible attraction for tourists and travelers fascinating the breathtaking Big Sur Coast. Whether you're seeking outdoor adventures, artistic inspiration, or a peaceful retreat by the sea, these two towns have something to offer every visitor.

Monterey Bay Aquarium

The Monterey Bay Aquarium, located on the attractive coastline of Monterey, California, is a fascinating and world-renowned attraction that beckons tourists and travelers to the stunning Big Sur Coast. settled between rugged cliffs and the azure waters of the Pacific Ocean, this iconic institution is a must-visit destination for nature enthusiasts, families, and anyone seeking a memorable marine experience.

Location and Setting: Perched at the edge of Monterey Bay, the aquarium enjoys a prime coastal location. As visitors approach, they are greeted by breathtaking views of the bay, with its rolling waves and abundant marine life. The aquarium's design seamlessly blends into the natural surroundings, creating a harmonious atmosphere that enhances the overall experience.

Exhibits: The Monterey Bay Aquarium boasts a diverse array of exhibits that showcase the rich marine biodiversity of the region. Visitors can embark on an underwater journey through exhibits like:

Kelp Forest: A towering underwater forest of swaying kelp fronds inhabited by sea otters, sharks, and a fascinating array of fish.

Open Sea: A colossal tank that houses awe-inspiring creatures such as tunas, sea turtles, and a variety of pelagic species, providing an immersive experience of the open ocean.

Tidepool Touch Tanks: Interactive touch pools that allow visitors to get up close and personal with tide pool inhabitants like sea stars and hermit crabs, providing a hands-on learning opportunity.

Jellies: Living Art: A fascinating display of jellyfish in a beautifully lit gallery, offering a serene and almost hypnotic viewing experience.

Penguin Habitat: Home to a playful colony of African penguins, this exhibit offers a chance to observe these pleasant birds both above and below water.

Conservation and Education: One of the aquarium's core missions is education and conservation. Informative displays, interactive presentations, and expert-led programs provide visitors with insights into marine conservation efforts and the importance of preserving our oceans.

Visitor Experience: The Monterey Bay Aquarium offers a seamless and enjoyable experience for all visitors. Amenities include a variety of dining options with scenic ocean views, a well-curated gift shop offering marine-themed souvenirs, and easily navigable facilities suitable for all ages and mobility levels.

Scenic Surroundings: After fascinating the aquarium, tourists can continue their journey along the breathtaking Big Sur Coast. The rugged beauty of the cliffs, the soothing sounds of the crashing waves, and the opportunity to spot whales and sea otters in their natural habitat make for an unforgettable coastal adventure.

The Monterey Bay Aquarium is a fascinating nearby attraction for tourists and travelers fascinating the Big Sur Coast. It combines a stunning coastal setting, diverse marine exhibits, educational experiences, and a commitment to conservation, making it a must-visit destination that both educates and inspires a deeper appreciation for the wonders of the ocean.

Cannery Row

Cannery Row is a pleasant and historic waterfront district located on the Monterey Peninsula, making it a popular nearby attraction for tourists and travelers fascinating the stunning Big Sur Coast. This vibrant destination offers a unique blend of natural beauty, cultural heritage, and recreational opportunities that make it a must-visit location.

Scenic Beauty: settled along the attractive shores of Monterey Bay, Cannery Row boasts breathtaking coastal views that provide a perfect backdrop for relaxation and exploration. The rugged cliffs of the

Big Sur Coast are just a short drive away, offering visitors the chance to experience the dramatic coastal landscapes that this region is renowned for.

Historical Significance: Cannery Row has a rich history rooted in the sardine-packing industry of the early 20th century. Visitors can dip themselves in this history by fascinating the Cannery Row Historic District, which includes preserved cannery buildings, antique machinery, and informative exhibits at the Pacific House Museum.

Unique Shopping and Dining: The row is lined with boutique shops, art galleries, and seafood restaurants. Visitors can indulge in fresh, locally caught seafood while savoring oceanfront dining experiences. Unique shops offer a wide range of souvenirs, art, and gifts, making it an excellent place to pick up a memento of your visit.

Outdoor Activities: Cannery Row offers various outdoor activities to enjoy the coastal surroundings. Kayaking, paddleboarding, and bike rentals are readily available for those looking to tour the bay and nearby coastal trails. It's also an ideal spot for wildlife enthusiasts, as sea otters, seals, and seabirds are often spotted along the shoreline.

Family-Friendly Attractions: Families with children will find the Monterey Bay Aquarium a fascinating attraction on Cannery Row. This world-class aquarium showcases diverse marine life, including fascinating displays of jellyfish, playful sea otters, and awe-inspiring sharks.

Events and Festivals: Throughout the year, Cannery Row hosts a variety of events and festivals, from art fairs to seafood festivals. These events provide a glimpse into the local culture and offer unique opportunities for entertainment and cultural enrichment.

Accessibility: Cannery Row's central location and proximity to other attractions, such as the 17-Mile Drive and Pebble Beach, make it a convenient base for fascinating the broader Monterey Peninsula and the Big Sur Coast.

Cannery Row is an enchanting destination that combines natural beauty, history, gastronomy, and recreational activities. It's an ideal stop for tourists and travelers fascinating the stunning Big Sur Coast, offering a memorable and diverse range of experiences that cater to a wide array of interests. Whether you're a nature enthusiast, history buff, or foodie, Cannery Row has something special to offer to enhance your visit to this breathtaking coastal region.

17-Mile Drive

17-Mile Drive is a renowned and attractive coastal route that beckons tourists and travelers to the stunning Big Sur Coast in California. This iconic stretch of road is a must-visit attraction, offering an unforgettable journey through some of the most breathtaking natural landscapes along the Pacific coastline. Here's description of 17-Mile Drive:

Sweeping Coastal Beauty: 17-Mile Drive is celebrated for its unparalleled scenic beauty, encompassing rugged cliffs, windswept cypress trees, and dramatic ocean vistas. The journey begins at the historic coastal town of Monterey, winding its way through the exclusive Pebble Beach community, and concluding at the pleasant town of Carmel-by-the-Sea. Along this route, travelers are treated to a visual feast of ever-changing coastal panoramas.

Golfers' Paradise: As you embark on this drive, you'll pass world-renowned golf courses, including Pebble Beach Golf Links. Golf enthusiasts flock to this area to witness the prestigious golf tournaments and the awe-inspiring fairways perched on cliffs overlooking the Pacific Ocean.

The Lone Cypress: One of the most iconic stops along the route is the Lone Cypress, a gnarled, weather-beaten cypress tree clinging tenaciously to a rocky outcrop. This symbol of resilience has become an emblem of the California coast.

Bird Rock: Bird Rock is another fascinating spot, known for its thriving seabird colonies. You can spot various species of seabirds, including cormorants and gulls, perched on the rocks and soaring gracefully above the waves.

Seal and Sea Lion Point: A favorite stop for wildlife enthusiasts, Seal and Sea Lion Point is where you can observe these marine mammals basking on the rocks or frolicking in the surf. The sight and sounds of these creatures are truly fascinating .

Spanish Bay: This inviting beach along the route is perfect for a relaxing stop. Visitors can stroll along the sandy shore, collecting seashells and taking in the tranquil ambiance.

17-Mile Drive Gatehouses: To access this coastal treasure , you'll need to pay a small fee at one of the gatehouses. However, the fee is well worth the experience, as it helps maintain the pristine environment and ensures an enjoyable visit for all.

Scenic Overlook Points: Throughout the drive, you'll find numerous scenic overlook points with interpretive signs explaining the geological formations, flora, and fauna of the area. These stops provide opportunities for stunning photographs and a deeper understanding of the local ecosystem.

Sundown Serenity: The drive is equally enchanting during the golden hours of sunrise and sunset. The shifting colors of the sky and the reflection on the ocean's surface create a magical atmosphere that photographers and romantics alike will appreciate.

17-Mile Drive is not merely a scenic route but an immersive experience that allows travelers to connect with the untamed beauty of the Big Sur Coast. Whether you're a nature enthusiast, a golf aficionado, or simply seeking serenity by the sea, this coastal drive is an essential stop for tourists and travelers fascinating   the California coast. It's a journey that leaves an indelible mark on the hearts and memories of all who venture along its winding path.

Wine Tasting in Carmel Valley

Big Sur Coast, Carmel Valley stands as a hidden treasure for wine enthusiasts and travelers alike. This tranquil valley is renowned for its vineyards and wineries, offering a delightful wine tasting experience that perfectly complements the natural beauty of the region. Here's a description of wine tasting in Carmel Valley as a nearby attraction for tourists and travelers fascinating the Big Sur Coast.

Scenic Beauty Meets Wine Excellence: Carmel Valley, situated just a short drive south of the iconic Big Sur Coast, welcomes visitors with its stunning vistas and idyllic countryside. As travelers venture into the valley, they are greeted by rolling hills, lush vineyards, and a serene atmosphere that provides an ideal setting for wine tasting. The valley's unique microclimate, characterized by warm days and cool nights, creates the perfect conditions for growing a variety of grapes, resulting in exceptional wines that capture the essence of the region.

Vineyards and Wineries Abound: Carmel Valley is home to a remarkable collection of boutique wineries and vineyards, each offering a distinct wine-tasting experience. Travelers can visit your family-owned estates and modern tasting rooms, all set against the backdrop of the Santa Lucia

Mountains. Notable wineries like Bernardus, Holman Ranch, and Folktale Winery & Vineyards showcase the finest in winemaking craftsmanship, featuring award-winning varietals that range from Chardonnay and Pinot Noir to Cabernet Sauvignon and Merlot.

Tasting Tours and Expert Guidance: For those seeking an immersive wine-tasting adventure, Carmel Valley offers a range of tasting tours and experiences. Visitors can embark on guided tours of vineyards to gain insight into the winemaking process, from grape to bottle. Knowledgeable staff and sommeliers are on hand to provide detailed descriptions of each wine's characteristics, allowing guests to refine their palates and discover their favorite varietals.

Al Fresco Dining and Pairing Perfection:

Many wineries in Carmel Valley offer al fresco dining options that pair their wines with locally sourced cuisine. Picture yourself savoring a glass of crisp Chardonnay while overlooking a vineyard, or enjoying a bold Cabernet Sauvignon with a gourmet picnic in the shade of towering oaks. These culinary experiences add an extra layer of delight to the wine-tasting journey, making it a complete sensory pleasure.

A Relaxing Retreat: Carmel Valley's wine-tasting scene isn't just about the wine; it's also about the relaxed and friendly ambiance. Visitors often find themselves in a community of fellow wine lovers, enjoying leisurely conversations, and unwinding amidst the vine-covered hills. The valley's slower pace is a welcome escape from the hustle and bustle of nearby urban areas, making it an inviting retreat for travelers.

Plan Your Visit: To make the most of your wine-tasting adventure in Carmel Valley, it's recommended to plan ahead. Check the operating hours and availability of tastings at your chosen wineries, and consider booking in advance, especially during peak tourist seasons. Additionally, if you're combining this experience with a trip along the Big Sur Coast, be sure to check road conditions and closures, as the route can be affected by weather and maintenance.

Wine tasting in Carmel Valley is an exquisite and harmonious blend of natural beauty, wine excellence, and hospitality. Whether you're a wine connoisseur or simply someone seeking a tranquil escape along the enchanting Big Sur Coast, this destination promises an unforgettable experience for your senses and your soul. Cheers to discovering the hidden treasures of Carmel Valley.

San Simeon and Hearst Castle

San Simeon and Hearst Castle are two iconic and must-visit attractions located along the stunning Big Sur Coast in California. This attractive region offers travelers a unique blend of natural beauty and historical grandeur.

San Simeon: San Simeon itself is a pleasant coastal town situated on Highway 1, approximately halfway between Los Angeles and San Francisco. It serves as the gateway to the world-renowned Hearst Castle and offers its own attractions for tourists.

Scenic Coastal Views: San Simeon boasts breathtaking coastal vistas, making it an ideal spot for leisurely strolls along Moonstone Beach or watching the fascinating sunset over the Pacific Ocean.

Coastal Wildlife: The area is known for its diverse wildlife, including elephant seals, sea otters, and various seabirds. Visitors can often observe these animals basking in the sun or frolicking in the surf.

Coastal Drive: The drive along Highway 1 in San Simeon is a highlight in itself, with winding roads that hug the rugged coastline, providing travelers with spectacular panoramic views.

Hearst Castle: Perched atop the Enchanted Hill overlooking San Simeon, Hearst Castle is a masterpiece of architecture and opulence, built by newspaper magnate William Randolph Hearst. Here's a detailed description of this historic Treasure :

Architectural Marvel: Hearst Castle is a sprawling estate consisting of multiple lavish buildings inspired by Mediterranean and Spanish Renaissance architecture. The main mansion, Casa Grande, is a palatial masterpiece adorned with exquisite art and antiques collected from around the world.

Art Collection: The castle boasts an unparalleled collection of art, including ancient statues, tapestries, and rare manuscripts. The opulent interiors feature ornate ceilings, grand libraries, and beautifully landscaped gardens.

Neptune Pool: One of the most iconic features of Hearst Castle is the Neptune Pool, a stunning Roman-inspired outdoor swimming pool with ornate statues and columns, surrounded by lush gardens and incredible views of the coastline.

Tours: Visitors can tourHearst Castle through guided tours that provide insights into the history of the estate, its art collection, and the fascinating life of William Randolph Hearst.

Scenic Grounds: The castle is set within a vast estate with manicured gardens and terraces. Roaming the grounds offers glimpses of exotic animals once owned by Hearst, like zebras and elk, which still graze freely.

Overall, San Simeon and Hearst Castle offer a fascinating blend of natural beauty, architectural splendor, and cultural richness that make them a must-visit destination for tourists and travelers along the Big Sur Coast. It's a journey through time and beauty that leaves a lasting impression on anyone fortunate enough to experience it.

Chapter Ten: Practical Information

Currency and Money Matters

When traveling to the stunning Big Sur Coast, it's essential to have a good understanding of currency and money matters to ensure a smooth and enjoyable trip. Here's a guide:

Currency: In the United States, the official currency is the United States Dollar (USD). Banknotes come in various denominations, including $1, $5, $10, $20, $50, and $100. Coins are commonly used for smaller transactions and are available in values of 1 cent (penny), 5 cents (nickel), 10 cents (dime), and 25 cents (quarter).

Currency Exchange: It's a good idea to exchange your home currency for USD before your trip or upon arrival at a bank, currency exchange office, or at the airport. While many businesses in Big Sur accept credit and debit cards, having some cash on hand for small purchases, tips, or places that may not accept cards can be helpful.

Credit and Debit Cards: Credit and debit cards are widely accepted throughout Big Sur. Visa and

Mastercard are the most commonly used, with American Express and Discover also accepted but to a lesser extent. To avoid problems when using your card, make sure to tell your bank about your plans to travel.

ATMs: ATMs (Automated Teller Machines) are readily available in Big Sur, especially in larger towns like Monterey and Carmel-by-the-Sea. One can withdraw cash using one's debit or credit card. Keep in mind that some ATMs may charge fees for out-of-network transactions, so it's a good idea to check with your bank.

Tipping: Tipping is customary in the United States, and it's an important part of the service industry. In restaurants, it's customary to leave a tip of 15-20% of the total bill for good service. In hotels, you may tip hotel staff, such as bellhops and housekeepers, as well. Additionally, it's common to tip tour guides, taxi drivers, and other service providers.

Sales Tax: Sales tax in California varies by location but is typically around 7.25% to 9.75%. This tax is added to the price of most goods and services at the point of purchase, so be prepared for this additional cost when shopping or dining out.

Mobile Payments: Mobile payment options like Apple Pay, Google Wallet, and Samsung Pay are widely accepted in many establishments, making it convenient to make payments using your smartphone.

Budgeting: Big Sur can be an expensive destination, especially when it comes to accommodations and dining. It's advisable to plan your budget carefully, considering not only lodging and food but also activities and transportation.

Currency Conversion Apps: To keep track of your expenses and easily convert currency, consider using currency conversion apps on your smartphone. These apps can help you stay within your budget and make informed spending decisions.

By keeping these currency and money matters in mind, you'll be well-prepared to tour the breathtaking Big Sur Coast while ensuring a hassle-free and enjoyable trip.

Sustainable Travel Practices

Sustainable travel practices for tourists or travelers visiting the Big Sur Coast are crucial to preserving the natural beauty and ecosystems of this stunning destination. Here's description of sustainable travel practices:

Plan Ahead: Before your trip, research and plan your itinerary. This helps minimize your impact on the environment by avoiding overcrowded areas and spreading out visitors' footprints.

Transportation: Opt for eco-friendly transportation options like hybrid or electric vehicles, carpooling, or public transportation. Big Sur's winding roads can be congested, so consider visiting during the offseason to reduce traffic.

Accommodation: Choose eco-friendly lodgings such as cabins, lodges, or hotels that implement sustainable practices. Look for certifications like LEED or Green Key, and consider staying at places that source their power from renewable energy.

Waste Reduction: Reduce waste by bringing reusable items such as water bottles, shopping bags, and containers for takeout food. Dispose of your trash responsibly in designated bins and consider participating in beach cleanup efforts.

Water Conservation: California faces periodic droughts, so use water sparingly in your accommodations and when hiking or camping.

Avoid activities that can pollute water sources, like washing dishes in streams.

Respect Wildlife: Admire wildlife from a distance and never feed them. Keep a safe distance from marine life, and if you're lucky enough to spot seals or sea lions, maintain a respectful distance of at least 100 feet.

Stay on Marked Trails: Stick to established hiking trails to prevent soil erosion and protect delicate ecosystems. Avoid shortcuts, as they can lead to irreversible damage to plant life.

Local Culture and Economy: Support the local economy by purchasing goods and services from local businesses. Learn about the culture and history of the area, and be respectful of the local communities.

Reduce Energy Consumption: Be mindful of energy use in your accommodations. Turn off lights, air conditioning, and heating when not in use, and open windows for natural ventilation whenever possible.

Wildfire Safety: Be aware of wildfire risks, especially during dry seasons. Follow fire safety guidelines, don't start campfires outside designated areas, and check for fire bans or restrictions.

Educate Yourself: Learn about the unique ecosystems, flora, and fauna of Big Sur. Understand the impact of your actions on these environments to make more informed decisions.

Group Size: Keep group sizes small when fascinating the wilderness. Smaller groups are less likely to disturb wildlife and ecosystems.

By following these sustainable travel practices, you can enjoy the unparalleled beauty of the Big Sur Coast while helping to protect and preserve it for future generations to enjoy. Remember that responsible tourism is key to maintaining the delicate balance of this remarkable natural environment.

Leave No Trace

Leave No Trace (LNT) is a set of principles that are essential for tourists and travelers visiting the stunning Big Sur Coast. LNT is all about minimizing your impact on the environment and preserving the natural beauty of this unique coastal region. Here's detailed description of Leave No Trace for visitors to Big Sur:

Plan Ahead and Prepare: Research and plan your trip in advance. Understand the local regulations and weather conditions.

Obtain any necessary permits and make camping reservations where required.

Pack appropriately for the season and terrain, ensuring you have all the essentials.

Travel and Camp on Durable Surfaces: Stick to established trails and campsites to avoid trampling on delicate ecosystems.

Camp at least 200 feet away from water bodies to protect water quality and wildlife habitat.

Use established fire rings or stoves for cooking and campfires where permitted.

Dispose of Waste Properly: Pack out all trash, litter, and leftover food. Leave no trace of your visit.

Use established toilet facilities when available. If not, bury human waste in a "cathole" at least 6-8 inches deep and 200 feet away from water sources.

Dispose of wastewater from cooking and cleaning at least 200 feet from lakes and streams.

Leave What You Find: Do not pick plants or disturb wildlife. Observe them from a respectful distance.

Leave rocks, flowers, and other natural and cultural features as you found them.
Respect historical and cultural sites, avoiding any damage or removal of artifacts.

Minimize Campfire Impact: Use a camp stove for cooking to prevent the depletion of firewood and minimize fire risks.
If campfires are allowed and there are established fire rings, keep fires small and use only small sticks and twigs.
Before leaving, ensure the fire is completely extinguished, and the ashes are cold to the touch.

Respect Wildlife: Keep a safe distance from animals, as approaching them can be harmful to both you and the wildlife.
Do not feed wildlife. Human food can be detrimental to their health and alter their natural behaviors.

Be Considerate of Other Visitors: Keep noise levels down, especially in wilderness and camping areas.
Yield the trail to others, and maintain a friendly and considerate attitude towards fellow travelers.
Keep pets on a leash and under control to prevent them from disturbing wildlife or other visitors.

Educate Yourself and Others: Share Leave No Trace principles with fellow travelers and encourage them to follow them.
Learn about the unique ecology, geology, and history of Big Sur to enhance your appreciation and understanding of the area.

By adhering to these Leave No Trace principles, you can help preserve the natural beauty and ecological integrity of the Big Sur Coast, ensuring that future generations of travelers can continue to enjoy this breathtaking destination. Remember, responsible tourism is essential for the long-term sustainability of our natural treasures.

Conservation Efforts

Conservation efforts by tourists and travelers in the Big Sur Coast region are crucial to preserving the area's natural beauty and fragile ecosystems. Here is description of some of these conservation efforts:

Leave No Trace Principles: Travelers to Big Sur are encouraged to follow the Leave No Trace principles. This means packing out all trash, including cigarette butts and food scraps, and leaving natural and cultural features as you found them. By doing so the impact on the environment is drastically reduced.

Responsible Camping: Tourists who camp in Big Sur should use established campgrounds and follow all campground regulations. Campfires are generally prohibited, so campers are encouraged to use camp stoves for cooking. This minimizes the risk of wildfires and reduces damage to the landscape.

Hiking Responsibly: Hikers are urged to stay on designated trails to avoid trampling on delicate vegetation and disturbing wildlife. Additionally, hikers should not pick plants, disturb animals, or leave behind any markers or graffiti.

Wildlife Observation: Tourists are encouraged to observe wildlife from a safe distance and avoid feeding them. Feeding wildlife can disrupt their natural behaviors and diets, leading to health issues and dependency on human food.

Sustainable Transportation: Travelers can reduce their environmental impact by carpooling or using public transportation to reach Big Sur. Once there, consider using eco-friendly transportation options like electric vehicles or bicycles for local travel.

Support Local Conservation Organizations:

Tourists can contribute to conservation efforts by donating to or volunteering with local environmental organizations focused on preserving Big Sur's unique ecosystems. These organizations often organize clean-up events and habitat restoration projects.

Educate Yourself: Travelers should take the time to learn about the specific conservation challenges facing Big Sur, such as erosion, invasive species, and wildfire risks. Understanding these issues can lead to more responsible behavior and support for local conservation initiatives.

Reduce Water Usage: Water conservation is vital in the drought-prone region of California. Tourists can conserve water by taking shorter showers, turning off taps while brushing teeth, and using water-saving fixtures in accommodations.

Proper Waste Disposal: Recycling and proper waste disposal are essential in reducing the impact of tourism on Big Sur. Visitors should make use of recycling bins and garbage disposal facilities to ensure waste is managed responsibly.

Respect Local Regulations: Travelers should familiarize themselves with local regulations and guidelines, such as fire bans and seasonal closures.

Compliance with these rules helps protect the environment and ensures the safety of all visitors.

By adhering to these conservation efforts, tourists and travelers can play a vital role in preserving the pristine beauty of the Big Sur Coast for future generations to enjoy while minimizing their ecological footprint.

Conclusion

As we wrap up this comprehensive travel guide to the stunning Big Sur Coast, it's clear that this remarkable stretch of California's coastline is a treasure trove of natural beauty and adventure waiting to thrill any tourist or traveler. Throughout this guide, we've meticulously explored the must-visit sites and attractions that define Big Sur's allure. Let's recap some of the highlights that should be on every traveler's itinerary:

Bixby Creek Bridge: The iconic gateway to Big Sur, this breathtaking bridge offers panoramic vistas of the rugged coastline. It's a photographer's dream come true.

McWay Falls: A secluded cove with an attractive waterfall that plugs directly into the Pacific Ocean, making it one of the most photogenic spots in the region.

Pfeiffer Big Sur State Park: An outdoor enthusiast's paradise, this park features redwood groves, hiking trails, and the chance to dip yourself in the region's rich flora and fauna.

Julia Pfeiffer Burns State Park: Home to the McWay Falls, this park also boasts numerous hiking trails, including the Ewoldsen Trail, which offers incredible views of the coastline.

Point Lobos State Natural Reserve: Known as the "Crown Jewel" of the California State Park system, this reserve offers dramatic seascapes, diverse wildlife, and excellent scuba diving opportunities.

Pfeiffer Beach: Famous for its purple-hued sands and dramatic rock formations, this beach is an ideal spot to relax, watch the sunset, and perhaps even spot migrating whales.

Nepenthe Restaurant: A dining experience with a view like no other, offering delicious cuisine paired with panoramic vistas of the coastline.

Big Sur Vineyards: For wine enthusiasts, this winery is a hidden Treasure that provides a taste of the region's unique terroir.

Hiking Adventures: Big Sur is a hiker's paradise with an array of trails, such as the challenging but rewarding Ventana Wilderness hikes and the more leisurely ones like the Pfeiffer Falls Trail.

Camping: Whether you prefer rugged wilderness camping or more developed campgrounds, Big Sur offers a range of options for sleeping under the stars.

Pfeiffer Beach: Famous for its purple-hued sands and dramatic rock formations, this beach is an ideal spot to relax, watch the sunset, and perhaps even spot migrating whales.

Local Art and Culture: Tour the local art galleries and cultural events that make Big Sur a unique destination, including the Henry Miller Memorial Library.

In conclusion, Big Sur Coast beckons travelers with its awe-inspiring landscapes, rich biodiversity, and a sense of tranquility that's increasingly rare in today's world. Whether you're an avid adventurer, a nature lover, or simply seeking a peaceful retreat, this guide has provided you with the essential information to make the most of your visit to Big Sur. From the towering redwoods to the crashing waves and the warm hospitality of the local community, Big Sur is an enchanting destination that will leave an indelible mark on your travel memories. So, pack your bags, embark on this unforgettable journey, and let the beauty of Big Sur Coast captivate your heart and soul.

Printed in Great Britain
by Amazon

37919654R00086